# Praise for *Seal the Deal*

Congratulations to Subhash Bhaskaran on the publication of his new book! Drawing from his years of experience in sales and business development, he has put together a valuable resource that reflects his expertise and insights. Having worked with him, I've seen his dedication and professionalism first-hand, and I'm sure this book will inspire and guide many. Wishing him great success!

– Vijay Deepak (Auckland, New Zealand), Business Development Manager, Röhlig Logistics

Having known Subhash for a long-time, I was always in admiration for his attention to details in listening and delivering, just what the clients want. His strength and strategy in terms of winning over people's hearts now being penned down in a book will definitely have for what it will take a novice to become a Ninja in Marketing & Sales. I am confident that this book will be a no-brainer for those who want to grow and shine in today's competitive world!

– Kaushik Kadir Muruganandam, Manager - HR, Corporate Functions, ELGi Equipments

# SEAL THE DEAL

## Close Sales Like a Pro!

SUBHASH BHASKARAN

JAICO PUBLISHING HOUSE

Ahmedabad Bangalore Chennai
Delhi Hyderabad Kolkata Mumbai

Published by Jaico Publishing House
A-2 Jash Chambers, 7-A Sir Phirozshah Mehta Road
Fort, Mumbai - 400 001
jaicopub@jaicobooks.com
www.jaicobooks.com

© Subhash Bhaskaran

SEAL THE DEAL
ISBN 978-81-990707-0-7

First Jaico Impression: 2026

No part of this book may be reproduced or utilized in
any form or by any means, electronic or
mechanical including photocopying, recording or by any
information storage and retrieval system,
without permission in writing from the publishers.

Page design and layout by Inosoft Systems, Delhi

Printed by
Thomson Press India Limited, New Delhi

# Contents

## Section III: THE EXECUTE PHASE



## SPECIAL SECTION

## Section IV: THE EVOLVE PHASE

# Acknowledgements

Writing this book has been quite the adventure, and it certainly wasn't a solo effort. I owe a huge thank you to the many people who've been part of this wild ride.

First and foremost, my deepest gratitude goes to my mentors, managers, and colleagues. Their wisdom, support, and occasional "constructive criticism" (let's call it that) have shaped the principles I've shared in this book. I've had the pleasure of learning from some of the best in the business—including a few bosses who, let's say, never missed an opportunity to really test my limits. Their shrewdness, tough love, and ability to ask for just a little more—when I thought I'd given it my all—helped shape me into the sales professional I am today. Thanks for keeping me on my toes (and slightly terrified)!

A special shoutout to my family and friends, who offered endless encouragement (and the occasional "Are you still working on that book?"). Your unwavering support gave me the confidence to tackle new challenges—even when the road seemed more like an uphill climb.

Lastly, to every salesperson out there hustling day in and day out: This one's for you. My hope is that this book becomes your trusted guide (and maybe even makes you chuckle once or twice) as you navigate the roller coaster that is sales.

Thank you all for being part of this journey—whether you knew it or not!

## SPECIAL THANKS

This is for the real VIPs in my life—those who've been right there through all the late nights, the work trips, and the endless sales calls.

**First and foremost, to my wife.** Let's be honest—this book wouldn't have been possible without your patience, support, and, well... endurance! You've had to make more sacrifices than anyone should, adjusting to my ever-changing schedule and sales demands. For all the missed dinners, interrupted weekends, and "I just need to take this one quick call" moments, I owe you big time. You're the real hero behind this book. Thank you for sticking with me through it all (and for not changing the locks on the door).

**To my dad**, thank you for teaching me the power of punctuality and commitment. You didn't need reminders, apps, or notifications to follow through on your word. If you said 9:00 AM, it was 9:00 AM—sharp. If you said a week, it meant a week—no excuses. These traits may seem simple, but in the world of sales, they are golden. Your values have been the foundation of my discipline and consistency.

**And to the Almighty**—thank you for guiding me through this roller coaster of a career, giving me strength, clarity, and purpose.

*This book is not just mine. It belongs to everyone who stood by me, believed in me, and pushed me forward—when I needed it the most.*

# Introduction

Sales is the lifeblood of any company. It is a journey filled with movement, unpredictability, and constant reinvention. Whether you're in a B2B or B2C organization, here's the unspoken truth—you can never settle.

No organization will ever say, **"You've closed enough deals; you can take it easy now."** Instead, the graph must rise, month after month, year after year. That's the rhythm of sales.

**Sales is an endless pursuit.**

What we achieve today may look impressive, but it is already history by tomorrow. Targets evolve, buyer expectations shift, and competitors get smarter. If you don't move forward, you're already behind.

And here's the reality of our times: Success in sales isn't just about persistence anymore. It is about evolution.

Whether you're a field-hardened sales veteran or someone just stepping into the arena, you'll agree that:

- The sales strategies of yesterday won't win deals tomorrow.
- Generic follow-ups, flat pitches, and repetitive scripts won't survive the modern buyer.
- And if you're not using technology like artificial intelligence (AI) to assist you, someone else will—and they'll win.

This book was born out of that urgency.

It is not just about closing deals—it is about closing deals smarter, faster, and with greater impact.

## WHAT YOU WILL LEARN IN THIS BOOK

This isn't a book filled with textbook theories. This is a battle-tested, real-world playbook. Whether you're handling enterprise software sales or walking into a retail showroom, whether you're closing five-figure deals or building funnels—this book has something for you.

### Inside, you'll discover:

- How to gather powerful insights from every lead using frameworks like SEDUCE;
- How to master negotiations with SNIPER-like precision;
- How to leverage AI tools to write sharper emails, personalize pitches, automate follow-ups, and stay ahead;
- How to deal with price wars, procurement traps, and buying committees;
- How to manage relationships, stand out, and still stay grounded; and

- How to turn emotional intelligence, storytelling, and even humor into secret weapons.

You'll also learn:

- Exercises to sharpen your strategy;
- Case studies that expose real sales wins and fails;
- Practical checklists and powerful formulas you can apply right away;
- The important fact that AI is not your enemy, but your biggest ally in this modern-day sales battlefield.

## Why I Wrote This Book

Because I know how it feels to chase a tough lead.

Because I've been on the other side of a negotiation where everything is on the line.

Because I've stared at a blank screen wondering how to reply to a client's tough email.

And most of all—because I've been helped, mentored, challenged, and inspired by the best. Now, it's time to give back.

This book is my version of mentorship—raw, honest, and shaped by real-life experiences.

It's written for every salesperson who wants to do more than just hit targets. It's for those who want to build a career, a reputation, and a legacy in sales.

So, whether you're just starting out, going through a dry patch, or looking to break into your next big role—this book is for you.

Let's evolve. Let's adapt. Let's win. Together.

And remember...

AI won't take your job. But a salesperson using AI might.

## THE SALESMAN'S PULSE: THE THRILL OF CONVINCING AND CLOSING

"Sales isn't just a job; it's the adrenaline that fuels every fiber of my being."

Before you dive into the strategies, formulas, and lessons this book offers, let me share something deeply personal—a glimpse into the mindset that drives me in sales. It is a place where passion meets purpose—where every conversation, every pitch, and every negotiation is charged with energy and purpose.

A close friend once asked me, "Why are you so drawn to sales? What makes you thrive in it?"

My answer was simple: *It's the thrill.*

I get an unexplainable rush when I see a prospect leaning in, their interest deepening, their resistance fading. That exact moment when someone genuinely begins to believe in what you offer is a feeling I chase again and again.

Convincing someone to invest their time, money, and trust in your offering is no small task. It's a psychological chess game, a moment of artful alignment. And when that moment culminates in a handshake, an agreement, a green light, it feels like victory. Not just for the deal, but for the effort, belief, and persuasion that led up to it.

Sales wasn't always just a profession for me. It started from a very raw and real place.

In my final year of engineering, my parents couldn't afford my academic fees because of financial challenges at home. I didn't give up. I went around the industrial belt of Tirupur, knocking on doors, presenting my case—not just asking, but *convincing*.

And one business owner saw something in me. He called me back the next day and handed me a demand draft for INR 10,000—no conditions, no expectations. He then introduced me to others in his circle. Soon, I had raised INR 50,000—just enough to complete my education.

That experience wasn't just about getting money. It was my first real taste of what selling truly is—presenting value, creating empathy, and building trust. That first "yes" gave me the same thrill I now feel every time I close a deal.

Sales, to me, is never just about the transaction. It's about *transformation.*

It's about building something meaningful with the person across the table. Every win isn't just about revenue—it's about impact.

So, remember this:

Sales is not just something you do. It's something you *live.* You must breathe it, own it, and let it spark that pulse within you.

If you've ever felt that electric moment when a deal turns in your favor, when the energy shifts in the room, when a prospect says, "Let's go ahead," then you know what I'm talking about.

And if you haven't felt that yet, don't worry.

By the time you reach the end of this book, I promise, you will.

## SALES-DRIVING PUNCHLINES

Before getting into the chapters, I want you, my dear reader, to absorb these punchlines to set the mood for this book. Read them twice or thrice to prepare yourself.

- *Sales is simple: Understand the client's problem and solve it better than anyone else.*
- *The best salespeople don't talk—they listen.*
- *Winners find a way to close, not an excuse to stop.*
- *When you steal momentum, momentum steals the results for you.*
- *You don't wait for opportunities—you create them.*
- *Your energy sells even before you open your mouth.*
- *Sales isn't about selling—it's about helping your clients win.*
- *The follow-up is your secret weapon.*
- *Don't just aim to hit targets—aim to surpass them.*
- *Adapt, evolve, and close the next big deal.*
- *Your pipeline is your lifeline.*
- *Confidence sells; hesitation doesn't.*
- *Great salespeople don't sell products—they sell solutions or results. (my favorite)*
- *Don't just pitch—prove your value.*

If any of these punchlines gives you food for thought, then you are ready to begin your journey into this book.

# 1

# The Foundations of Sales Mastery

"Sales is simple: Understand the client's problem and solve it better than anyone else."

Sales is often misunderstood as a pure numbers game, but the truth is that sales is a unique blend of science and art. Studies suggest that 80% of sales is science—a structured, methodical process that can be learned and replicated, while the remaining 20% is art—the creative ability to read people, adapt to different personalities, and build meaningful relationships. Mastering both is what differentiates great salespeople from good ones.

## SALES: 80% SCIENCE, 20% ART

At its core, sales follow a systematic process: prospecting, qualifying leads, making presentations, handling objections, and closing deals. This is the "science" of sales—the part that can be measured, optimized, and improved through data and best practices. This part is about understanding the steps and moving through them efficiently.

And then, there's the "art"—the ability to navigate human emotions, build trust, and adapt to the personalities of the people you're selling to.

No two prospects are the same. Each client you interact with comes with their own character, mindset, and unique set of challenges. This is where the magic happens.

### Scenario: The Salesperson's Challenge

Imagine interacting with a wide variety of people every day. One moment, you're talking to a high-energy, fast-paced decision-maker who wants to know the numbers. The next moment, you're dealing with a cautious, methodical client who needs time to process every detail. Yet, you're the same salesperson—adapting, connecting, and bringing value to each unique personality.

Ask yourself:

- How can I hone my skills to deal with a diverse range of personalities while still being authentic?
- What creative approaches can I use to tailor my style to each prospect, ensuring I build trust and close the deal?

### The Science of Sales: Process and Precision

The science of sales is about perfecting your process. Every great salesperson follows a defined cycle, which we will deep dive into in the upcoming chapters:

- Prospecting: Finding the right leads
- Qualifying: Determining who has the need, authority, and budget to buy
- Presenting: Clearly communicating the value you bring
- Handling objections: Overcoming the hurdles and concerns
- Closing the deal: Sealing the agreement with confidence

This process is repeatable and measurable. The more you refine it, the more effective you become. It is about precision—knowing what to say, when to say it, and how to handle each stage with confidence.

## THE ART OF SALES: THE HUMAN ELEMENT

The art of sales brings life to this process. Think about it: No two interactions are the same. Each prospect you meet has their own personality—whether they're decisive, analytical, outgoing, or reserved, your ability to connect with them on their level is what makes the difference.

This is where empathy, adaptability, and emotional intelligence come into play.

Successful salespeople know how to read the room, adjust their tone, and engage in a way that makes their prospects feel understood and valued.

## WHY SALES IS EXCITING

Sales isn't just a job; it's an adventure. Every day brings new challenges, people, and opportunities to build relationships. The excitement lies in the fact that no two deals are ever the same. You work with a mix of personalities—sometimes you'll deal with straight-talkers, and at other times, with those who need a little more time and reassurance. But in the end, it's you who adapts, pivots, and finds ways to get the deal done.

## MASTERING BOTH THE SCIENCE AND THE ART

To truly excel in sales, you need to master both the science and the art. This mastery means being consistent and methodical in your process while being adaptable and creative in your interactions. Think of it like playing a musical instrument: You learn the technical aspects (science), but it's your personal flair and improvisation (art) that create a memorable performance.

## EXERCISE: REFLECT AND BUILD

Take a few minutes to reflect on your recent sales experiences. Ask yourself these questions, and jot down your thoughts:

- Who was your last successful client?
- How did you build trust with them?
- What made the relationship work?
- Was there a turning point that moved the deal forward?

Think of a deal you lost recently.

- Was it due to a lack of rapport or a missing personal connection?

- What could you have done differently to build more trust or add more value?

### Action Step: Revisit Your Relationship-Building Approach

Over the next week, focus on building deeper relationships with your clients.

Schedule a call or send a thoughtful email that's not about selling—just connect with them personally.

Reflect on how this step impacts your relationship and any deals in progress.

Remember, sales success is built on relationships. The more trust you cultivate, the easier closing the deal becomes.

## THE 4E FRAMEWORK: A SALESPERSON'S JOURNEY

To make this book actionable and easy to navigate, I've structured it around the **4E Framework**—a practical model I developed to capture the complete sales journey.

| Stage | What It Covers |
|---|---|
| **Explore** | Handling leads, qualifying prospects, mapping personas, and understanding customers |
| **Engage** | Customizing demos, pre-indoctrinating prospects, building rapport, and managing partners |
| **Execute** | Submitting proposals, handling objections, negotiating smartly, and closing with confidence |

| | |
|---|---|
| **Evolve** | Growing with emotional intelligence (EQ), execution quotient (XQ), AI adoption, ethics, humor, personal branding, and mastering the monk mindset |

This framework doesn't just reflect theory—it mirrors how real salespeople succeed in the field. Each chapter in this book falls under one of these four categories, so you always know where you are in your journey and what muscle you are developing.

# Section I

# THE EXPLORE PHASE

# 2

# Handling Leads—The First Step to Success

"The best salespeople don't talk—they listen."

In sales, everything begins with a lead. Leads are the lifeblood of your sales pipeline, but not every lead will turn into a sale. That's why your approach to handling leads can make or break your sales process. The first step to success in any deal is a structured, disciplined approach to handling leads, fueled by research, organization, and your trusted customer relationship management (**CRM**) system to track your progress.

## THOROUGH INVESTIGATION: WHO IS THE LEAD?

Before diving into any conversation, you need to do your homework. Leads aren't just names or numbers; they represent individuals and companies with unique needs, challenges, and goals. Understanding who the lead is, what their company does, and how your product can provide value to them is the foundation of any successful sales effort.

To truly understand a lead, you need to research:

- **Who is this lead?** What is their role in the company, and are they the decision-maker?
- **What does the company do?** What are its core products or services?
- **What challenges might the company be facing in its industry?**

Use online resources like **LinkedIn**, the company's website, and any relevant industry news for your research. By gathering this information, you can start building a narrative around how your product or service fits into your lead's world. Remember, this stage is about **genuine conversations** with the lead—not just relying on data, but engaging with them to discover more about their needs.

### Scenario: Be the Detective

Imagine being handed a lead with just the name and contact information. The lazy way is to jump right into a cold pitch, hoping something sticks. But that's not what successful salespeople do. Instead, you take the time to research—visit LinkedIn, explore the company's latest news, and read up on industry trends. You find a challenge the company is facing that your product could solve. Armed with this knowledge, your approach is no longer generic—it is personalized and targeted, because you put in the extra effort.

Ask yourself:

- How often do I invest enough time in understanding a lead before I make contact?
- How can I build genuine conversations with leads to discover more about their needs?

## The Urge to Gather Information: Discovering the Full Picture

We go to great lengths to get what we want in everyday life.

When we're on the hunt for the best food, we're willing to travel miles or try a dozen different places just to get that perfect meal.

When we're looking for a movie to download or the latest viral video we missed, we search every platform and every link until we find it.

For that perfect gift for a loved one, we don't stop until we find something meaningful.

And let's not forget the time you *really* wanted the contact number or Insta ID of your crush—you didn't rest until you had it, did you?

So, here's the point: when it comes to **looking for information about a lead**, that same level of **enthusiasm**, **curiosity**, and **restlessness** needs to kick in. You have to approach lead research like it's a quest for the best food, the perfect song, or even that contact number you've been dying to get. The more information you gather, the more prepared you are, and the better your chances of success.

## ORGANIZING YOUR LEADS: THE BACKBONE OF YOUR PROCESS

Once you've done your research and engaged in conversations, the next step is **organizing your leads**. A scattered approach to lead management is a recipe for disaster. This is where having a solid **CRM system** becomes essential—not for insights, but for tracking every action you've taken, recording the steps, and making sure you never lose sight of where each lead is in the sales process.

A typical CRM process should involve categorizing leads as follows:

- **Hot Leads:** Ready to move forward and likely to convert soon
- **Warm Leads:** Interested, but need more nurturing
- **Cold Leads:** Not yet ready or a lower priority

Your CRM will allow you to track email conversations, set reminders for follow-ups, and record every interaction. Handling leads isn't just about gathering information; it's about **documenting** and **managing** that information effectively.

### Nurturing Leads: Building Trust From Day One

Once your leads are organized, the next critical step is **nurturing** them. Every interaction you have with a lead is an opportunity to build a relationship, establish trust, and showcase your value. The key here is consistency—following up on time, sharing relevant information, and most important, **listening** to what they need.

Many salespeople make the mistake of pushing for a quick close. But here's the truth: Leads don't want to feel like just another deal. They want to know that you're invested in solving their problems. That's why nurturing is a crucial part of your sales process.

## EXERCISE: INVESTIGATE, ORGANIZE, AND NURTURE

### Research the Lead Using Online Sources

- Visit LinkedIn, company websites, and industry news.
- Have a conversation with the lead to discover their needs.

### Organize Your Leads in the CRM

- Are they a hot, warm, or cold lead?
- What actions have you taken, and what follow-ups are needed?

### Nurture the Relationship

- Schedule follow-ups in your CRM based on what stage the lead is in.
- Use your findings to send personalized emails or make tailored calls that add value for the lead.

## CLOSING THOUGHT

Leads aren't just opportunities—they are the start of a journey. By setting up a process, following it, and using your CRM as a tool to track your actions, you can handle leads in a way that sets you up for success from the very beginning. The more thoughtful and organized your approach, the greater the likelihood of closing the deal down the road.

# 3

# Qualifying the Leads: Separating Prospects From Suspects

"Winners find a way to close, not an excuse to stop."

Once you've gathered your leads and started engaging with them, the next critical step is **qualification**. Not every lead will be a good fit for your product or service, and it is essential to identify the ones that are worth pursuing. This is where you separate the **prospects**—those likely to convert—from the **suspects**—those who might be only browsing or aren't ready to move forward. Proper lead qualification saves time and energy, and it ensures that your efforts are directed toward closing the right deals.

## THE IMPORTANCE OF LEAD QUALIFICATION

Qualifying leads requires you to ask the right questions to determine whether the lead is a viable opportunity. As exciting as it may be to see a long list of potential clients in your pipeline, not all of them will be ready to buy—nor will everyone be the right fit. By qualifying leads early, you can prioritize your efforts, streamline your process, and focus on closing deals that have the highest potential.

### Scenario: The Overloaded Pipeline

Imagine you have a huge pipeline of leads, and it feels like you're on top of the world. But as you dive deeper, you realize most of these leads aren't serious prospects. They don't have the budget, the need, or the authority to make decisions. If you keep focusing on everyone equally, you'll burn out chasing deals that will never close.

Ask yourself:

- What if you spent your time only on the leads who are genuinely ready to buy?
- How much more effective could you be if you knew whom to prioritize?

### From Lead to Opportunity: The Conversion Point

A lead officially becomes an **opportunity** once you submit a proposal. But the journey from lead to opportunity involves the following crucial stages, each of which lays the foundation for the proposal:

- **Initial Research and Contact**: Understanding the lead's business, pain points, and goals (covered in **Chapter 2**)

- **Engagement and Qualification**: Asking the right questions to determine if they are a fit (this chapter)
- **Building the Relationship**: Nurturing the lead through meaningful interactions and follow-ups (to be covered in **Chapter 4**)
- **Tailoring the Proposal**: Crafting a solution that directly addresses their needs and pain points (covered in future chapters)

Converting a lead into an opportunity doesn't happen overnight. It is the result of deliberate and thoughtful interactions at each stage. Only when you've gathered enough information and built a relationship based on trust can you confidently submit a proposal and mark that lead as a true opportunity.

## THE QUALIFICATION PROCESS: *BANT* AND BEYOND

A common framework for qualifying leads is the **BANT** method, which focuses on four key criteria:

- **Budget**: Does the lead have the financial resources to purchase your product or service?
- **Authority**: Is the lead the decision-maker, or do they need to consult someone else?
- **Need**: Does the lead have a clear need for your solution?
- **Timeline**: Is there a defined timeline for when they plan to make a decision or purchase?

While BANT is a solid foundation, sales today requires going beyond these basics. **Dig deeper into the lead's needs—**

understand their pain points, their goals, and how your solution fits into their long-term plans. Don't just check boxes; engage in conversations that uncover the full picture.

### Tip: Go Beyond the Basics

Qualifying a lead isn't about filling out a checklist—it is about understanding their **story**. Ask questions that reveal more than just budget or authority. Find out what challenges they face and what success looks like for them. Qualifying leads means thinking strategically about how you can be the solution to their biggest problems.

## RED FLAGS: WHEN TO MOVE ON

As you qualify leads, it is important to know when to walk away. Not every lead will be a fit, and that's okay. Watch out for **red flags** that indicate a lead may not be worth pursuing, such as:

- **No clear budget**: If the lead has no idea how much they can spend, they may not be ready to decide yet.
- **Lack of urgency**: If the lead is interested but has no timeline for buying, it might be better to follow up later.
- **Unclear authority**: If you're not speaking to the decision-maker or the lead can't connect you with one, you may be wasting your time.

Recognizing these signs early can save you from chasing dead-end deals.

## EXERCISE: QUALIFY AND CONVERT YOUR LEADS

### Review Your Current Leads

- Use the BANT framework to determine if they're worth pursuing.
- Are they ready to move forward, or do they need more time?

### Engage Meaningfully

- Make sure your interactions help build a relationship that leads to a proposal submission.

### Recognize When a Lead Becomes an Opportunity

- When you're ready to submit a proposal, that's when your lead has truly converted into an opportunity. Make sure you've laid the groundwork for this step forward.

### CLOSING THOUGHT

Qualifying leads isn't about having the most names in your pipeline—it is about having the right names. By focusing on the leads that are a good fit and ready to buy, you will not only close more deals but also do so more efficiently. Remember, the real winners in sales are the ones who focus on the right opportunities, not just the most opportunities.

# Section II

# THE ENGAGE PHASE

# 4

# Tailoring the Demo or Presentation to the Prospect's Industry

"Sales isn't about selling—it's about helping your clients win."

A one-size-fits-all approach to sales presentations does not work in today's business landscape. Every prospect is unique, and so are their needs. To make an impact, you must **tailor your demo or presentation** to align with the specific industry, challenges, and goals of the prospect. This personalized approach builds trust, demonstrates your understanding of their world, and increases the chances of closing the deal.

## UNDERSTANDING THE PROBLEM STATEMENT AND VALUE PROPOSITION

Before tailoring your presentation, your goal is to **understand the problem statement**. What specific challenges is your prospect facing? What keeps them up at night? Your demo should directly address these pain points with a clear **value proposition** that shows how your solution will solve their problem.

It is essential to position yourself not as a product seller, but as someone who offers **results** and **solutions**. You're not just pitching a product; you're showing how your solution can transform the prospect's business by solving real problems and delivering measurable outcomes.

### Tip: Sell Results, Not Products

When presenting to a prospect, avoid focusing on the product itself. Instead, focus on the **results** the product will deliver. Clients don't want to hear about features; they want to know how those features will **solve their problems** and **drive success**. You're not just selling products; you're selling a **solution** to a challenge they're actively facing.

### Scenario: A Tailored Approach vs. a Generic Pitch

Imagine you're selling the same software to two companies: one in the healthcare sector and the other in retail. A generic presentation that doesn't consider their unique challenges will fall flat. However, by tailoring your demo to address the **specific pain points** of each industry—such as compliance regulations for healthcare or supply chain management for retail—you will immediately show value. The healthcare company sees how your software could help them manage patient data securely, while the retail company understands how it could improve inventory management.

Ask yourself:

- How can I adjust my presentation to address the specific pain points of each prospect?
- What industry-specific examples can I use to demonstrate value?

### Customizing the Demo: Address The Prospect's Pain Points

When you conduct a product demo, don't just showcase features; **demonstrate how your solution solves the prospect's specific pain points**. Make sure the value proposition is clear and targeted—emphasize how your solution delivers **results**, not just a product.

Consider these examples:

- If your prospect's problem is operational inefficiency, show them how your solution saves time and streamlines processes.
- If their challenge is customer retention, demonstrate how your solution improves the customer experience and boosts satisfaction.

This approach will show that you've not only done your homework but that you're also invested in **solving their problem**, not just selling a product.

### Tip: Be Selective With Features

Not every feature of your product is relevant to every prospect. Tailor your demo to focus on the features that will have the most significant impact on their business.

For example, if you're presenting to a finance company, emphasize features that enhance data security and streamline compliance. If you're presenting to a manufacturing company, focus on features that improve operational efficiency.

### Use Case Studies and Industry-Specific Success Stories

One of the most powerful ways to tailor a presentation is to include **case studies** or **success stories** from companies in the same industry. This approach demonstrates that your product has already worked for others facing similar challenges and gives the prospect confidence that it can work for them too.

When possible, use real-world examples to show the impact of your solution for other clients. Be specific—talk about measurable outcomes like cost savings, efficiency gains, or improved customer satisfaction.

### Tip: Make It About Them, Not You

A common mistake in demos is spending too much time talking about your company, your product, and its features. Remember, the presentation is about **helping the client win**, not showing off what you can do. Keep the focus on how your solution will help them achieve their goals.

## EXERCISE: TAILOR YOUR NEXT DEMO

### Research the Prospect's Industry

- What are the top challenges in their industry?
- How does your product solve those challenges?

### Select the Most Relevant Features

- Narrow down your demo to the features that will have the most impact on this prospect.
- Customize your message to align with their goals.

### Incorporate Case Studies

- Use industry-specific examples or case studies to show the real-world impact of your solution.
- Be ready to answer how your product helped others in the same field.

### CLOSING THOUGHT

Tailoring your demo or presentation is the key to showing prospects that you understand their world and are invested in their success. By focusing on their specific challenges and goals, and demonstrating how your solution aligns with their needs, you set yourself up to win the deal. Remember, **sales isn't about selling—it's about helping your clients win**.

# 5

# Gathering Key Information

"Your pipeline is your lifeline."

The process of gathering essential information from a prospect is one of the most critical stages in sales. Before you can confidently submit a proposal, you need to have a clear understanding of the **budget**, **timeline**, and other key factors that will influence the decision-making process. This is where preparation, relationship-building, and thorough inquiry come into play.

## INTRODUCING THE *SEDUCE* FORMULA

To simplify this process and make it easier to remember, let's introduce the **SEDUCE** formula. This approach will help you cover all the critical bases when interacting with a prospect, ensuring that you get the information you need while building a strong relationship.

Here's how **SEDUCE** breaks down:

### S: Solution-Focused

Always frame your conversation around solving the prospect's problem. You're not selling a product—you're offering a solution that directly addresses their challenges.

### E: Engage and Explore

Ask open-ended questions to **engage** with the prospect and **explore** their needs. Dig deep to uncover pain points and understand their goals.

### D: Discover Decision-Makers

Identify who holds the decision-making power. Are you speaking to the right person, or do you need to involve someone else to move forward?

### U: Understand the Urgency

Gauge how urgent the prospect's need is. Is there a pressing issue they need to solve immediately, or are they exploring options for future purchases?

### C: Clarify the Budget

Always ensure that you're clear on the prospect's financial constraints. Discussing the budget openly prevents misunderstandings later and allows you to tailor your offer accordingly.

### E: Establish Value

Finally, emphasize the unique value your solution brings. It's not just about offering features—it's about **proving** how your solution will deliver results.

By following the **SEDUCE** formula, you'll make sure you're gathering all the essential information while keeping the conversation focused on solving the prospect's problem.

## WHEN TO SUBMIT THE PROPOSAL: THE RIGHT TIMING

Submitting a proposal is a significant step in the sales process, and it should only be done when you're **fully convinced** that your solution is the right fit. Before sending out a proposal or commercial offer, ensure that you have gathered and clarified all the key parameters, such as:

- **Budget**: Make sure the financials align and there is no ambiguity.
- **Timeline**: Understand when the prospect plans to make a decision or implement the solution.
- **Mode of Purchase**: Clarify whether the prospect is interested in subscription, perpetual licensing, or another model.

It is crucial to submit the proposal only when you're confident that these factors are aligned. Rushing a proposal without having clarity on these aspects can lead to missed opportunities or an ill-fitting offer.

## BUILDING RAPPORT: THE BRIDGE TO KEY INFORMATION

To gather essential information and insights from the prospect, you need to build a strong **rapport** from the very first interaction. This relationship-building creates a bridge where the prospect feels comfortable enough to share inside information freely with you. When prospects trust you, they will be more likely to express their pain points, share detailed requirements, and even share insights into internal decision-making processes.

This level of openness can be achieved only if you have the talent to communicate effectively, **speak well**, and make the prospect enjoy speaking with you. Your conversational skills are the key to unlocking valuable information. Without building this trust, prospects may withhold critical details, leaving your proposal and solution misaligned with their needs.

### Scenario: A Deal at Risk

Imagine you're about to send a proposal, but you're unsure about the budget or who exactly will make the final decision. If you send the proposal without this information, you risk either pricing yourself out of the deal or losing momentum because the proposal isn't reviewed by the right person. However, by using the **SEDUCE** formula and building rapport early on, you gather everything you need up front, ensuring that your proposal is both targeted and timely.

## EXERCISE: USE THE *SEDUCE* FORMULA

- **Solution-Focused**: How can your product solve the client's problem? What results are they looking for?
- **Engage and Explore**: What key pain points can you uncover through your conversation? What are your prospect's goals?
- **Discover Decision-Makers**: Are you speaking to the decision-maker, or do you need to involve someone else?
- **Understand the Urgency**: How pressing is their need? Do they have a set timeline?
- **Clarify the Budget**: What is the financial range for this project?
- **Establish Value**: What unique value can you offer that differentiates you from competitors?

### CLOSING THOUGHT

Gathering key information is the backbone of any successful proposal. By using the **SEDUCE** formula, you can ensure that you collect all the necessary details while building a strong relationship with the prospect. Remember, **your pipeline is your lifeline**, and the more information you gather, the stronger that pipeline becomes. And never forget—submit your proposal only when you are fully convinced that your solution is the right fit and the parameters for timing are aligned.

# Section III

# THE EXECUTE PHASE

# 6

# Brainstorming for Submitting Commercials

"Don't just pitch—prove your value."

After understanding the prospect's specific pain points and gathering the key information—budget, timeline, and key decision-makers—the next step is to **brainstorm** and craft the perfect commercial offer. To create a winning deal, you need to dig deeper than just putting numbers on a proposal. **Brainstorming as a group** is essential because it brings together multiple perspectives, leading to a more refined, strategic offer that aligns perfectly with the prospect's needs and your business goals.

## WHY GROUP DISCUSSIONS AND BRAINSTORMING ARE ESSENTIAL

In sales, the pressure to close deals often pushes individuals to rush through the proposal process. However, when you take the time to **collaborate** with your team through brainstorming, you unlock new ideas, reveal hidden opportunities, and identify potential risks that you may have overlooked on your own. Here are a few reasons why group discussions are crucial:

## DIVERSE PERSPECTIVES LEAD TO STRONGER PROPOSALS

Each team member brings their unique experience and knowledge to the table—whether it is understanding pricing models, knowing the technical requirements, or having insights into customer behavior. This diversity **helps to create** a more comprehensive proposal that considers multiple factors.

### Spot Potential Red Flags

Group discussions can help you catch potential issues early, such as pricing too low or missing key features the client may need. By discussing these elements openly, you can avoid mistakes and ensure that your commercial offer is competitive yet realistic.

### Refining the Value Proposition

As a group, you can collectively brainstorm the best ways to articulate the value of your solution. Having different viewpoints ensures you highlight the most impactful aspects of your proposal that might not be obvious to a single person. This process makes sure the client understands why your solution is worth the investment.

### Ensure Alignment Across Departments

Often, your proposal requires input from multiple departments—finance, technical, legal, and marketing. Brainstorming allows everyone to **align on key aspects** of the offer, such as pricing strategies, service levels, or implementation timelines. It ensures that no surprises arise later.

### Creating a Flexible, Client-Centered Proposal

Brainstorming provides ideas for how to make your proposal more **client-centric**. Can you offer different pricing models, flexible payment plans, or additional support services that make your offer more attractive? Group discussions encourage creativity, leading to a solution that better resonates with the client's needs.

### Boosting Your Proposal-to-Win Ratio

By gathering as much information as possible and putting it through a thorough brainstorming session, you greatly increase the chances of winning the deal. This process not only helps you craft a proposal that aligns with the client's needs but also boosts your **proposal submitted vs. orders won** percentage. The more prepared and strategic you are, the better your win rate will be.

## SETTING THE STAGE: THE INPUTS FOR BRAINSTORMING

Before diving into the proposal, you need a clear set of inputs to help you make strategic decisions about pricing and offer structure. The brainstorming process should be grounded in detailed discussions around the following factors.

**Cost Structure**: What is the actual cost of delivering your solution? Include not just the basic product or service cost, but also the hidden costs, such as after-sales support, onboarding, customization, and maintenance.

**Client's Perceived Value**: What is the **value** the client sees in your solution? Is it high-impact, solving a major pain point, or just a small improvement? The more critical your solution is to the client's business, the more room you have for flexibility in pricing.

**Competitor Pricing: Research competitor pricing** and evaluate how your solution compares in terms of features, support, and overall impact. This comparison helps you determine whether to price higher (if you offer more value) or to match the market with added benefits.

**Long-Term return on investment (ROI) for the Client**: How will your solution impact the client's business in the long run? Emphasize measurable results, such as cost savings, operational efficiency, or increased revenue. When clients see the long-term ROI, they are more likely to invest at a higher price point.

**Client's Budget**: Understand the client's budget from your previous discussions. How can you align your pricing to match their financial constraints while still delivering value?

## PRICING STRATEGY: FINDING THE BALANCE

When brainstorming for pricing, you need to strike a delicate balance. Your pricing should be neither too low (undermining your product's value) nor too high (scaring away the client). But how do you decide whether to quote higher or lower than the actual cost?

### When to Quote Higher

If your solution is **mission-critical** to the client's success or delivers substantial long-term ROI, you can afford to quote higher. The key is to show how your solution solves high-impact problems.

If your competitors offer fewer features or lower-quality service, you can quote higher based on your **superior value**.

If the client has a **larger budget**, they may be willing to pay a premium for a solution they perceive as top-tier.

### When to Quote Lower

If you sense the client has **budget constraints**, quoting lower might make sense to get your foot in the door. However, ensure this lower quote does not compromise profitability. Offer a **scaled-down version** of your solution if needed.

When you're dealing with a **price-sensitive market**, quoting lower can help you gain market share. This approach is only sustainable if you can make up for the lower price in volume or future upselling opportunities.

### When to Stay at Market Price

If your solution is **comparable** to others on the market but offers additional benefits, match your pricing to industry standards and emphasize the **extra value** you provide. Make sure the client sees why choosing you at market price is still the better deal.

### Why and Why Not? The Decision-Making Process

During brainstorming, always ask: **Why should we quote this price? Why not go higher or lower?** These questions force you and your team to justify every decision, ensuring that your proposal is strategically sound. Here are some considerations to think about:

#### Why quote higher?

- Will the client get long-term savings that justify the investment?
- Is there a strategic benefit (e.g., market leadership or cutting-edge technology) that sets your solution apart?

#### Why quote lower?

- Are you entering a new market where winning the deal is more important than immediate profitability?
- Will quoting lower lead to future opportunities, such as additional services or greater upselling potential?

#### Why not quote lower?

- Would lowering the price **devalue** your solution in the eyes of the client?

- Could a lower quote hurt your profitability, leading to financial strain for your company?

## THE IMPACT: CREATING A WIN-WIN SITUATION

A successful commercial offer is one where both you and the client feel like you've won. You should be happy with the margins, and the client should feel that they're getting exceptional value for their investment. Here's how to ensure a **win-win**:

**Demonstrate Impact**: The client should see the **immediate and long-term impact** of your solution, whether it is cost savings, efficiency improvements, or increased profitability.

**Justify the Investment**: Make sure you justify every part of the pricing in terms of the value delivered. Whether you're quoting higher or lower than the standard rate, explain why your solution is worth the investment.

**Highlight the long-term ROI** that goes beyond short-term gains.

**Offer Flexibility**: Provide different pricing models (subscription, perpetual, tiered) or **multiple options** so that the client can choose what fits their needs and budget. This flexibility shows that you are solution-focused and are not just trying to sell.

## EXERCISE: BRAINSTORM YOUR NEXT COMMERCIAL

- **Review Your Inputs**: Gather detailed insights about cost, the client's perceived value, competitor pricing, long-term ROI, and the client's budget.
- **Strategically Adjust Pricing**: Decide whether to quote higher, lower, or match the market. Ensure that every pricing decision is justified based on value.
- **Build a Win-Win Offer**: Structure your proposal so both your company and the client feel like they're getting a great deal. Include flexibility and long-term benefits to create a winning partnership.

### CLOSING THOUGHT

Brainstorming isn't just a formality—it is a critical step that helps you think strategically about pricing, offer structure, and value. By collaborating with your team, you ensure that no stone is left unturned and that your proposal delivers maximum impact. **Don't just pitch—prove your value** by submitting a proposal that makes both your company and the client feel like they've won.

# 7

# Presenting the Proposal: Tailoring It to the Prospect

"A great salesperson doesn't sell products—they sell solutions or results."

After gathering all the essential information, brainstorming, and crafting a winning commercial offer, the next critical step is to **present** the proposal to the prospect. Presenting isn't just about delivering a well-designed document—you need to communicate the value your solution brings. At this stage, your role shifts from that of a **salesperson** to a **consultant**. It's time to show the prospect that you're not just selling them a product; you are offering a solution tailored to their unique needs, and ultimately, to the **results** they're looking for.

## ACT LIKE A CONSULTANT, NOT A SALESPERSON

When presenting a proposal, it's important to adopt a **consultative approach**. Think of yourself as a trusted advisor, guiding the prospect toward the best possible solution to their problems. You're not there to push a product—you are offering them a way to overcome their challenges and achieve their goals.

Being consultative means:

- **Listening more than talking**: Even during the proposal presentation, take the time to ask questions and listen to the prospect's feedback.
- **Solving their problems, not pushing your agenda**: Your goal is to provide value by solving your prospect's specific problems. Frame your presentation around how your solution addresses their pain points.
- **Offering insights and advice**: As a consultant, your expertise should shine through. Offer insights into how they can implement your solution effectively and the benefits they'll see.

### Tailoring the Proposal to the Prospect's Needs

The key to a successful proposal presentation is **personalization**. This is not the time for generic pitch decks or canned presentations. Everything you say should reflect the specific needs of the prospect. Here's how to tailor the proposal:

**Revisit Their Pain Points**: Start by reminding the prospect of the key challenges they shared with you during your earlier conversations. This recap immediately shows them that you've been listening and that your proposal is based on their needs.

**Present Your Solution as the Answer**: Frame your solution as the direct answer to the problems they're facing. Show how each feature or service you're offering is specifically designed to address their pain points and meet their goals.

Use clear, simple language to explain the **results** they can expect from your solution. Don't get bogged down by technical details—focus on the outcomes.

**Provide Multiple Options**: Whenever possible, offer **multiple options** or **tiers** in your proposal (e.g., basic, premium, custom). This approach shows flexibility and gives the prospect the ability to choose a solution that fits their needs and budget.

Make sure each option highlights the **added value** they get as they move up the tiers.

**Break Down Costs Into Smaller Components**: When presenting the total cost, **break it down into smaller components** to make the overall price feel more digestible. For example, instead of showing the total cost up front, show how much each specific feature or service costs. This breakdown makes the investment seem less overwhelming while highlighting the value of each component.

By breaking down the costs, you give the prospect a clearer picture of where their money is going and how each part of your solution contributes to solving their problems.

**Highlight ROI and Long-Term Benefits**: Emphasize not just the immediate benefits but also the **long-term ROI** they will experience. Help them see how your solution will provide lasting value, making the investment worthwhile over time.

Include tangible metrics—cost savings, efficiency improvements, or revenue growth—if possible. These metrics help to justify the investment.

## SENDING A COMPELLING COVER EMAIL

When submitting your proposal via email, never underestimate the power of a **compelling cover email**. This communication is your first touchpoint, and it can set the tone before the prospect even opens the proposal. Make sure the email:

- **Reinforces your consultative approach**: Recap the pain points you discussed and how your proposal addresses them.
- **Highlights key aspects of the proposal**: Mention the main solution and benefits briefly to pique their interest.
- **Creates a sense of urgency or momentum**: Encourage them to review the proposal soon, and express your eagerness to discuss any questions or concerns.

A strong cover email positions you as a proactive and attentive partner, making the prospect more likely to engage with the proposal.

## THE ART OF PRESENTATION: IT'S NOT ABOUT YOU

While it's tempting to spend time talking about your company's successes, awards, and history, remember: **The proposal is not**

**about you—it's about the client.** Keep the focus squarely on how your solution solves their problem. Here's how to stay client-focused:

**Start With Their Needs**: Make the proposal entirely about them, starting from the very first slide or page. Talk about their industry, their challenges, and the specific pain points they've shared with you.

**Avoid the Features Dump**: Resist the urge to overload the prospect with every feature of your product. Instead, focus only on the features that directly solve their problems, and explain how these features will make a difference.

**Engage, Don't Lecture**: Turn the presentation into a **conversation**, not a lecture. Ask questions to check for understanding, seek feedback, and ensure that the prospect feels heard throughout the process.

**Be Prepared for Objections:** No matter how well you tailor the proposal, there will likely be objections. Don't shy away from them—embrace them as opportunities to further engage with the prospect.

Common objections may include:

- **Budget Constraints**: Be prepared to explain the ROI and offer flexible pricing models.
- **Timing Concerns**: Address any timeline worries by demonstrating how your solution can be implemented efficiently.

- **Comparisons to Competitors**: Be ready to show how your solution offers superior value or better long-term benefits.

The key to handling objections is to maintain a **consultative tone**. Don't argue—guide the prospect through the objection and show them why your solution still stands as the best choice.

### Scenario: Acting as a Consultant

Imagine you're presenting a proposal to a prospect in the manufacturing sector. Instead of jumping into a long feature list, you begin by revisiting the pain points they shared with you—operational inefficiencies, high costs, and slow production cycles. You then present your solution as the answer to these specific problems, showing how your product will streamline operations and reduce costs over time. During the presentation, you ask questions to check whether these are still the primary concerns, and you adjust your proposal based on their feedback.

Ask yourself:

- Did I clearly present my solution as the answer to their unique problems?
- Did I take the role of a consultant by guiding them through the decision-making process?

## EXERCISE: TAILOR YOUR NEXT PROPOSAL PRESENTATION

- **Revisit Their Pain Points**: How well do you understand the prospect's challenges? Are you tailoring the proposal to address their specific pain points?
- **Focus on Results**: Present your solution as the **answer** to their problems and focus on the results they will achieve.
- **Prepare for Objections**: Think of the most likely objections and plan how you will respond to them in a consultative manner.

## CLOSING THOUGHT

Presenting a proposal is more than just reading through a document. It is an opportunity to act as a **trusted advisor** and show the prospect how your solution can transform their business. By taking a consultative approach and focusing on their specific needs, you create a deeper connection and increase your chances of closing the deal. Remember, **a great salesperson doesn't sell products—they sell solutions or results.**

Special Section

# Imagine Yourself in These Scenarios. Are You Ready to Be the X-Factor?

Before we dive into the next stages of the sales process, let's take a moment to reflect on the impact a great salesperson can have. **Sales is not just a profession; it is an opportunity to make a lasting difference**—for your company, your clients, and yourself. Here are five scenarios to inspire you to think about how you can become the X-factor in your organization and in your sales career.

### Scenario 1: Becoming the X-Factor

Imagine you're working for a company facing a tight financial year. The organization is relying heavily on closing a few critical deals to make it through the quarter. You're in the final stages of presenting a proposal, and the pressure is on to win this one. By taking a consultative approach—focusing on how your solution can help the client succeed—you're not just saving the deal, you're saving the company's financial year.

Ask yourself:

- Could I be the salesperson who makes that difference for my company by acting as a true consultant?

### Scenario 2: Turning Objections Into Opportunities

During your proposal presentation, the prospect raises concerns about pricing and how it fits into their budget. Rather than seeing this concern as a roadblock, you view it as an opportunity to offer insights and flexibility. By breaking down costs and focusing on how your solution will meet their needs, you turn the objection into a discussion that strengthens your position and helps build trust.

Ask yourself:

- Am I prepared to handle objections by guiding the prospect and offering value-driven solutions?
- How can I use objections as a way to build deeper trust and strengthen the proposal?

### Scenario 3: Becoming the Highest-Paid Salesperson

Imagine closing deal after deal by consistently taking the consultative approach—understanding your prospects' pain points, offering tailored solutions, and presenting proposals that hit the mark. Over time, your performance sets you apart, and you become the highest-paid salesperson in your company, even surpassing some leadership roles. This is the power of acting as a **trusted advisor** rather than just a salesperson.

Ask yourself:

- Could I position myself as a top performer by consistently delivering consultative, results-driven proposals?
- What would it feel like to become the go-to salesperson in my organization, known for closing critical deals?

### Scenario 4: Saving the Deal in a Crunch Situation

Imagine the company you work for is struggling to close its financial year with positive numbers. The leadership is counting on just one or two deals to push them over the line, and time is running out. You step into the proposal presentation with the confidence that your consultative approach will not only win the deal but also save the company from falling short of its financial targets. By understanding the client's needs and addressing objections effectively, you close the deal that saves the year.

Ask yourself:

- What steps can I take to ensure I'm the salesperson who delivers when it matters most?
- How can I leverage my skills as a consultant to guide prospects toward a positive decision under pressure?

### Scenario 5: Overcoming a Performance Slump

Imagine you've had a tough few months. Deals have been slipping through your fingers, and you're feeling the pressure to perform. The fear of not hitting targets is looming large. Instead of giving in to the slump, you decide to reset your approach. You reconnect with your **consultative mindset**, digging deeper into understanding each prospect's unique needs. Slowly but surely, you begin closing deals again, and you not only recover but also surpass your targets. Your resilience and adaptability turn a difficult situation into a massive success story.

Ask yourself:

- How can I bounce back from a tough quarter by shifting my approach?
- What steps can I take to reconnect with the fundamentals and come out stronger?

**TAKE A MOMENT TO REFLECT**

Sales is about more than just hitting targets. It is about rising to the occasion when it matters most. Whether you're saving your company in a crunch situation, overcoming objections, or becoming the highest-paid salesperson, each scenario demonstrates how sales professionals can make a lasting impact.

I won't give you the answers to these scenarios here. **That's the purpose of this book.** Read on, and you'll figure out how to tackle these situations and become the X-factor in your sales career.

# 8

# The Follow-Up: Your Secret Weapon

"The follow-up is your secret weapon."

For many salespeople, the submission of the proposal feels like the finish line. After multiple rounds of calls, demos, presentations, gathering requirements, brainstorming, and refining the commercial offer, it is tempting to feel like the job is done once the proposal is in the client's inbox. In reality, **this is where the most critical phase begins**. The effort you put into following up and driving the proposal **toward** closure is what differentiates great salespeople from good ones.

## DON'T RELAX YET—THE REAL WORK STARTS NOW

It is natural to feel a sense of relief after submitting a proposal. You've put in the hard work, and now it is out of your hands, right? Wrong. This is where many salespeople go wrong by easing up too early. While you might feel that the heavy lifting is done, the truth is that your most effective approach needs to start **after** the proposal is submitted.

By this stage, you've already invested significant time and energy into the opportunity. You've researched the lead, given demos, gathered detailed requirements, and fine-tuned your offer. **All of this effort is wasted if you don't drive the proposal to closure**. Submitting the proposal is just one step—now, you need to stay on top of it with a strategic follow-up plan.

## WHY FOLLOWING UP IS CRITICAL TO CLOSING THE DEAL

Following up is often seen as a basic task, but it is an essential part of moving a proposal from submission to signed contract. Prospects rarely make decisions immediately after receiving a proposal. They might have concerns, questions, or internal discussions to navigate. Without a structured follow-up process, your proposal risks becoming lost in their inbox.

Here's why follow-ups matter more than ever at this stage:

- **Keeps you top of mind**: Prospects are busy, and your proposal could get lost in the shuffle. Following up ensures that you stay relevant and visible throughout their decision-making process.
- **Helps clarify any doubts**: Following up gives you the chance to address any concerns or questions the prospect didn't initially raise. It's a perfect opportunity to engage them in a more detailed discussion.

- **Shows commitment**: Following up shows the prospect that you are committed to helping them and that their business matters to you. It builds trust and reinforces your professionalism.

## HOW TO FOLLOW UP STRATEGICALLY

Effective follow-ups are about balance. You want to stay engaged without overwhelming the prospect. Here's how to follow up without seeming pushy:

**Set the Stage Early**: Even before you submit the proposal, set expectations about your follow-up. Let the prospect know you'll check back in a few days to answer any further questions they may have. This establishes a natural flow for communication.

**Don't Overwhelm, but Don't Disappear**: After submitting the proposal, give the prospect a little breathing room, but don't vanish. Send a light follow-up email within a few days, checking in to see if they've had a chance to review and if they need any clarification.

**Add Value in Every Follow-Up**: Each follow-up should offer something useful. Whether it's additional information, answering a question, or sharing an industry insight that might be helpful, you want to make sure each touchpoint adds value. Avoid generic "just checking in" emails, and give the prospect a reason to stay engaged.

**Use Appropriate Chat Mediums**: Following up doesn't have to be limited to email or phone calls. You can use any chat medium that the prospect prefers based on their region and convenience. Whether it's WhatsApp, LinkedIn, or other chat apps, a quick message after sending the proposal can make a big difference. For example, you can send a message like, "Hey [Prospect], I've just sent the proposal—let me know if you have any questions."

Not all follow-ups should be solely about getting an update on the proposal. You can follow up on the pretext of discussing other relevant topics, like recent clients you've won, a similar client you're currently working with, or new product launches that may interest the prospect. This way, your follow-up conversation stays meaningful and distinct from what your competitors might be doing.

**Build Rapport for Easier Follow-Ups**: Following up should feel natural to both you and the prospect. If you've built a strong rapport during the lead stage, demos, and discussions, your follow-ups will feel like a continuation of that conversation rather than an intrusive request for an update. A good relationship established early on will make the prospect more open to your follow-ups.

**Encourage the Next Step**: Every follow-up should aim to advance the conversation. Whether you're requesting feedback, proposing a follow-up meeting, or asking for clarification on next steps, make sure you're always guiding the prospect toward moving forward in the decision-making process.

### Scenario: The Follow-Up That Sealed the Deal

Imagine you submitted a proposal for a large corporate client, and a week later, you still haven't heard anything. Instead of waiting in silence, you send a friendly follow-up email offering to clarify any points from the proposal and share an additional insight about how your solution can improve their process. You follow up with a quick message via the chat medium they prefer, confirming you've sent the email and offering assistance. The prospect replies, raising concerns about a specific feature. You take the opportunity to provide additional details, easing their concerns, and propose a meeting to discuss implementation timelines. That follow-up, paired with the added value, nudges the deal toward closure.

Ask yourself:

- Am I following up in a way that adds value and keeps the conversation moving?
- How can I turn my follow-ups into opportunities to address concerns and build trust?

## AVOIDING COMMON FOLLOW-UP PITFALLS

Follow-ups are powerful, but only if you do them right. Here are some common mistakes to avoid:

**Being Too Aggressive**: No one likes being pressured. Be persistent, but maintain a respectful tone and give the prospect space when needed. **A company or manager should never push sales teams to follow up aggressively**, as this can damage the relationship and make prospects uncomfortable.

**Following Up Without a Purpose**: If your follow-ups don't add value or offer something new, they risk becoming annoying. Make sure every touchpoint moves the conversation forward.

**Ignoring Prospects' Responses**: If a prospect raises concerns or questions, address them directly in your follow-up. Don't send generic responses or ignore important feedback.

### EXERCISE: BUILD YOUR FOLLOW-UP PLAN

- **Think of a recent proposal you've submitted**: What is your current follow-up strategy? Have you given the prospect a reason to stay engaged with each follow-up?
- **Create a multi-step follow-up plan**: Plan out two or three different follow-ups that offer new insights, ask relevant questions, or address potential concerns.
- **Use diverse follow-up methods**: If you've been relying on email, try a phone call, chat message, or LinkedIn message for your next follow-up.

### CLOSING THOUGHT

The follow-up is where deals are often won or lost. You can't afford to relax after submitting a proposal—this is where the real effort begins. With strategic, value-driven follow-ups, you'll guide the prospect from proposal submission to closure. Remember, **the follow-up is your secret weapon** for closing the deal and securing long-term success.

9

# Negotiation and Closing: The Final Strike

"Winners don't wait for perfect moments—they shape them with precision and confidence."

Negotiation and closing are not separate stages. They are two halves of the same powerful strike that determines whether your effort turns into revenue or remains just another "almost." If qualifying is about understanding, demos about showing, and proposals about aligning, then negotiation and closing are about sealing the value and walking the talk.

These moments demand preparation, patience, clarity ... and courage.

## NEGOTIATION: THE ARENA OF TRUTH

### 1. Preparation Is Your Superpower

Every successful negotiation starts long before the actual conversation. Don't wing it. Prepare the following:

- What is your lowest acceptable price?
- What value additions can you offer without losing margins?
- What are the possible objections, and how will you counter them?

Always conduct a pre-call huddle with internal stakeholders (sales lead, legal, finance, technical) to prepare for the negotiation.

### 2. Know What Happens if There's No Deal

This possibility is important for both sides.

What will it cost your company if this deal doesn't close?

More important, what happens to the *prospect* if the deal falls through?

Framing this possibility clearly allows you to confidently highlight your solution as *indispensable,* not optional.

### 3. Negotiate the Process First

Ask:

- "Who will be involved in making the decision?"
- "Are there any internal reviews or approvals needed?"
- "What does your procurement cycle look like?"

You'll prevent last-minute surprises.

### 4. Don't Just React—Ask Why

If the prospect says, *"This price seems high,"* ask, *"What are you comparing it against?"* or *"What part of the proposal feels misaligned with your expectations?"*

Uncovering the *why* gives you leverage.

### 5. Present the First Offer and Tell a Story

Anchor the negotiation. Don't just say, *"INR 5 lakh."* Say, *"We arrived at INR 5 lakh based on your need for XYZ modules, 1-year support, and scalable licensing."*

This explanation gives context and avoids the "plucked-from-thin-air" perception.

### 6. Label Your Concessions

Instead of "We can give you 10% off," say, "We typically don't offer this discount, but we're doing it to kickstart a long-term relationship."

Show that your concession is a strategic move, not desperation.

## CLOSING: WHERE IT ALL COMES TOGETHER

After negotiation, the transition into closing must be seamless. **Closing is not about pressure—it is about clarity and timing.**

### 1. Recognize Buying Signals

"When can we start?"
"Can you include this clause in the agreement?"
"We've internally discussed your proposal ... "
These statements are green lights—go for the close!

### 2. Closing Techniques You Must Master

#### a) Assumptive Close:

"Let's schedule the kickoff next week—Monday or Tuesday?"

b) Summary Close:

"We've covered ROI, integration, and onboarding. Can we move forward with the final paperwork?"

c) Direct Close:

"Are you ready to proceed?"
Choose what suits the situation—but **don't delay.**

### 3. What To Do After Closing

**Send a Summary Email**: Recap deliverables, payment terms, and timelines.

**Make a Smooth Handoff**: Pass details to implementation without friction.

**Stay Engaged**: Don't disappear. A short WhatsApp message or email after three days can mean a lot.

## THE SNIPER FORMULA FOR CLOSING A DEAL: YOUR SECRET WEAPON

| Letter | Represents | What To Do |
|---|---|---|
| S | Set the Stage | Prepare and position with clarity. |
| N | Negotiate the Process First | Understand timelines and stakeholders. |
| I | Identify Key Motives | Ask why, not just what. |

| P | Present the First Offer | Anchor it with a well-framed quote. |
|---|---|---|
| E | Empathize With Constraints | Understand the limitations and adapt. |
| R | Respond Thoughtfully | Use objections to deepen the conversation. |

## REAL-WORLD SCENARIO: STANDING TALL AGAINST PROCUREMENT

In the upcoming pages, you will read my **Success Story: Turning the Tables—Keeping Procurement on the Back Foot Without Losing the Deal.** I encountered a procurement team from a leading Indian bank who tried to push me to waive the software license cost completely—because they were a "big name."

## CLOSING EXERCISE

Identify a live deal you're handling. Write down:

- The prospect's biggest objection;
- Your counter-offer strategy (without slashing price); and
- Your preferred closing style (assumptive, summary, or direct).

Practice it. Rehearse it. Seal it.

### CLOSING THOUGHT

The deal isn't won when the demo goes well—it is won when you negotiate with precision and close with confidence.

Don't just reach the finish line. **Cross it with grace, assertiveness, and control.**

# 10

# The Sales Journey: A Quick Recap

"Every step matters, but the journey is ongoing."

We've covered the core steps of the sales process, from handling leads to closing deals. Each chapter so far covered an essential building block in mastering the art of sales. Whether you're a seasoned professional or new to the world of sales, following these steps systematically ensures you are well prepared to navigate the complexities of each opportunity.

## STEP-BY-STEP RECAP

### Handling Leads

The foundation of any sales process starts with identifying and handling leads. It is not just about gathering names and contacts—it is about understanding the prospect's industry, challenges, and objectives.

### Qualifying Leads

Not every lead is worth pursuing. Qualifying leads helps you focus on those that have the right budget, fit, and need for your product or service. This step is crucial for maximizing your efforts and ensuring you don't waste time on prospects who won't convert.

### Tailoring Presentations

A well-crafted presentation speaks directly to the client's pain points. We explored how tailoring presentations based on the prospect's needs is key to showing that your solution solves their specific problems.

### Gathering Information

Sales isn't just about pitching—it's about listening. Gathering key information, such as the budget, decision timelines, and client expectations allows you to create an offer that aligns with your prospect's needs.

### Brainstorming for Commercials

The internal process of brainstorming for pricing and proposals ensures that the offer you put on the table is strategic, competitive, and meets both your goals and the client's.

### Negotiation

Negotiation is where you align your offer with the client's expectations. We covered various strategies, including handling objections, managing concessions, and the importance of understanding the process before discussing terms.

### Closing the Deal

Closing is often where salespeople hesitate, but it is the most critical stage. Techniques such as recognizing buying signals, using the right closing approach, and confidently guiding the prospect toward a decision are what make the difference between a lost opportunity and a win.

### Post-Closing Steps

Once the deal is closed, the relationship doesn't end—it evolves. Ensuring smooth implementation, staying involved, and building trust after the sale sets the stage for long-term success.

## WHERE DO WE GO FROM HERE?

The journey through the sales process is not a linear one—it is iterative. Each step builds upon the last, but it is important to remember that sales is a dynamic field. The strategies that worked yesterday may need to be refined today, and the skills you've learned will continue to evolve as you encounter new challenges.

Now that we've laid the foundation, it's time to dive deeper into more specialized topics. Whether it is mastering negotiation techniques, handling partnerships, or developing the resilience needed to thrive in high-pressure sales environments, the next chapters will explore the nuances that will take your sales game to the next level.

## CLOSING THOUGHT

Every step in the sales process is important, but the journey isn't over yet. As we move forward, remember that sales is as much about adaptability and creativity as it is about following a process. So, let's take what we've learned, build on it, and dive into the next phase of becoming a true sales leader.

# 11

# Who Is an Ideal Salesperson?

"Great salespeople don't sell products—they sell solutions and results."

When we talk about the qualities of an ideal salesperson, it's not just to do with how they interact with clients or prospects. The ideal salesperson also plays a critical role within their organization, contributing to the success of the entire team. Let's break these qualities down into two parts: **internal qualities** (how they operate within the organization) and **external qualities** (how they engage with clients, prospects, and partners).

## THE IDEAL SALESPERSON WITHIN THE ORGANIZATION

### Team Player, Not a Lone Wolf

Sales might feel like a solo mission at times, but the best salespeople understand that success comes from **collaboration**. Whether it is working with marketing to align messaging or involving the technical team for product support, an ideal salesperson knows how to pull in the right resources at the right time.

### Clear Communication With Cross-Functional Teams

A good salesperson doesn't just communicate well with clients—they know how to keep their internal teams in the loop. This communication involves sharing updates, providing clear instructions, and ensuring everyone understands the status of the deals in progress. Transparent communication within the organization helps avoid unnecessary delays and confusion.

### Consistency and Reliability

Your organization should trust you to deliver, whether it is keeping the CRM updated, meeting deadlines, or following through on internal processes. An ideal salesperson is known for their **reliability**—they consistently execute and deliver without needing constant oversight.

### Mentorship and Sharing Knowledge

Great salespeople lift others up. By sharing insights, strategies, and learnings with colleagues, they help **raise the overall performance** of the team. This sharing doesn't mean giving away all your secrets, but offering guidance and advice to those who can benefit from your experience.

### Adaptability to Feedback

Within their organization, a strong salesperson is open to **feedback** and willing to adjust their approach when necessary.

This ability to take constructive criticism, adapt to new strategies, and implement company-wide changes is a hallmark of someone committed to continuous improvement.

## THE IDEAL SALESPERSON WITH CLIENTS, PROSPECTS, AND PARTNERS

### Maintain a Low Profile: Reduce the Hype

Clients appreciate salespeople who are genuine, not over-the-top talkers. The ideal salesperson doesn't rely on hype or over-selling. Instead, they **focus on the client's needs** and how their solution solves real problems. Staying humble builds trust and keeps the conversation centered on the value you bring.

### Calmness Is Key: Stay Cool Under Pressure

Being calm in high-pressure situations is a superpower. Prospects often need to make significant decisions, and they don't need a salesperson who adds stress to the process. Staying calm, composed, and on an even keel—even when things get tense—reassures clients that you're in control and have their best interests in mind.

### Listen Actively and Respond Thoughtfully

Listening isn't just a passive activity—it is the most important part of any sales interaction. The ideal salesperson doesn't interrupt or jump ahead. They listen carefully to understand the client's real needs and challenges, and then respond thoughtfully. **Listening more than talking** is a key part of building a strong client relationship.

### Personalize Interactions Through Memory

People love to feel remembered. When you remember a small personal detail—whether it is your prospect's favorite coffee or a story they shared—it shows that you're paying attention and genuinely care. These details can make a huge difference in establishing long-term relationships.

### Follow Up Thoughtfully

Follow-ups are critical in sales, but there's a right way to do it. Instead of being pushy, a great salesperson checks in thoughtfully. For instance, sending a message like, "I hope everything is okay—I haven't heard from you in a while and just wanted to check in," shows that you care about the person, not just the deal.

### Adapt and Learn from Every Interaction

No two clients are the same, and an ideal salesperson knows how to adapt their approach to each situation. Whether the prospect prefers a more formal interaction or a relaxed chat, you need to **adapt to their communication style**. This flexibility makes it easier to build rapport and trust.

### Have a Sense of Humor and Be Authentic

Having a **sense of humor** goes a long way in sales. It humanizes the interaction and can defuse tension in tricky situations. An ideal salesperson knows how to lighten the mood without being unprofessional. Humor helps prospects feel more at ease, making the sales process smoother.

## Build a Network of Friendly Prospects

The best salespeople don't just build a one-time relationship—they create a **circle of trust**. By building relationships that go beyond the deal, they create a network of prospects and partners who stay connected even as they move to new companies. These relationships can turn into long-term opportunities.

## Scenario: Balancing Internal and External Excellence

Imagine this situation: You've just secured a major deal with a high-value client. Internally, the sales team is celebrating your win, but now you need the operations and technical teams to deliver on time. However, they're swamped with other projects and can't prioritize your new client. How do you handle this situation?

Externally, the client is eager to move forward and is relying on you to ensure everything goes smoothly. They trust you, but delays could jeopardize the relationship you've worked so hard to build. Do you push your internal team to prioritize this client at the risk of straining internal relationships? Or do you communicate openly with the client, managing their expectations while finding a way to balance both sides?

Ask yourself:

- How can I maintain my role as a trusted partner externally while being a team player internally?
- How do I communicate with both the client and my internal team to ensure the project gets done without damaging relationships on either side?

# 12

# Who Should Choose a Career in Sales?

"Sales isn't just a job—it is a dynamic journey of growth and opportunity."

Not everyone is cut out for sales, but for those who are, it offers one of the most rewarding career paths in any industry. So, who should consider a career in sales? Let's break it down. A career in sales is for individuals who possess the following traits:

## THRIVE ON CHALLENGES

Sales is full of challenges—whether it is securing a new client, overcoming objections, or hitting your targets. If you enjoy tackling obstacles head-on and finding solutions, then sales could be the right fit for you. It is a career where your drive and determination are constantly tested, but the rewards match the effort.

### LOVE INTERACTING WITH PEOPLE

If you're a **people person**, you'll likely enjoy sales. Building relationships, understanding client needs, and delivering value are all about connecting with people. If human interaction energizes you and you enjoy forming new connections, you're already on the path to becoming a great salesperson.

### ARE RESULTS-ORIENTED

In sales, your success is measured directly by the results you achieve. If you thrive in environments where your efforts can be quantified—whether it is through hitting sales targets, earning commissions, or closing deals—sales offers a unique blend of performance and reward.

### ARE SELF-STARTERS WHO WANT CONTROL OVER THEIR EARNINGS

One of the biggest draws to a sales career is the potential for **unlimited earnings**. If you're a self-starter who doesn't want to be confined by a fixed salary, sales gives you the freedom to control your income. The harder and smarter you work, the more you can earn.

### VALUE PERSONAL GROWTH

Sales is not just about numbers—it is about personal growth. The skills you learn, such as negotiation, persuasion, and relationship management, are transferable across industries and roles. If you value continuous learning and want a career that pushes you to grow, sales offers endless opportunities for self-improvement.

## CLOSING THOUGHT

Sales is a journey of growth and opportunity. An ideal salesperson strikes the perfect balance between being a valuable contributor within their organization and being a trusted partner to clients and prospects. Internally, they collaborate, communicate, and help the team succeed. Externally, they are calm, adaptable, and focused on building long-term relationships. For those who are driven by challenges, love interacting with people, and want control over their earnings, sales is a career that offers limitless growth and reward.

# 13

# The Attitude One Should Possess in Sales

"Winners find a way to close, not an excuse to stop."

Sales isn't just about the product or service you offer—it's about **you**. Your attitude, approach, and how you carry yourself can make all the difference in closing a deal. In every interaction, you're not only selling your product, but you're also competing with other skilled salespeople, each trying to win the prospect's attention. So, how do you stand out?

### 1. Understand the Competition: Salesperson vs. Salesperson

When a prospect has a requirement, they're likely speaking to both you and your competitors. Your competitors also have skilled, tactical salespeople vying for the same deal. It's not just **product vs. product**—it's **you vs. them**. Your communication, the way you engage, and how you treat the prospect should make them feel that among all the vendors, you're the **best**. And you need to be the best **every time**. You can't afford to let that drop, not even for a moment.

### 2. Do Justice to Every Lead

Now, take a look at your leads and opportunities. Ask yourself, **"Have I done justice to every lead I'm handling?"**

It's not just about numbers on a spreadsheet—it's about ensuring that you've given every lead the attention, care, and strategic thinking it deserves. Every lead is a potential win, and treating each one with importance keeps you sharp and focused. A great salesperson knows that every interaction counts, and they bring their best to every conversation.

### 3. The Salesperson's Impact Can Outshine the Product

A good salesperson can **boost the impact** of a product, even if it's not the best on the market. On the other hand, a poor salesperson can **kill a deal** even if the product is superior. The attitude you bring to the table—whether it is confidence, energy, or empathy—has the power to make or break the deal. Never underestimate your influence in the process. In sales, you're not just representing a product; you're representing yourself as the best choice to the prospect.

### 4. Preparation Is Key: Stay Ahead in the Race

Sales isn't just about showing up—it's about showing up **prepared**. You have to think about every possible way to position yourself ahead in the race. From understanding the prospect's needs to anticipating their objections, your preparation will keep you ahead of the competition. It's not just about product vs. product—it is salesperson vs. salesperson. When you prepare thoroughly, you set yourself apart. In this game, the person who is **more prepared and more strategic** will win the deal.

### 5. Disconnect the Prospect From Competitors

A smart salesperson knows how to **disconnect** the prospect from their competitors. This doesn't mean bad-mouthing others; it means **owning the relationship** and positioning your solution in such a way that the prospect naturally gravitates toward you. Remember, you can't underestimate the prospect—they are savvy, and they know they have other options. Your job is to make them feel that even though those options exist, the deal should still be awarded to you.

### 6. Bring the Prospect to Your Zone

Master bringing the prospect into **your zone**—a space where they feel comfortable, engaged, and confident in your offering. You have to subtly guide the prospect away from considering others and make them feel that your solution is the one they've been looking for. This is where the real skill of a salesperson shines—being able to make the prospect **choose you** without feeling pressured.

## CLOSING THOUGHT

Your attitude sets the tone. In sales, your attitude isn't just a part of the equation—it **sets the tone** for the entire process. From seeing the competition as a challenge to ensuring you're the best option for the prospect, the right attitude will not only help you close deals but also build long-lasting relationships. Be strategic, stay calm, and always bring your best to the table. Success in sales isn't just about the product—it's about how you carry yourself every step of the way.

14

# Importance of Personal Branding for Salespeople

"Your personal brand is the story people tell about you when you're not in the room."

In sales, personal branding is more than just creating a professional image—it involves building trust, credibility, and a lasting impact that transcends each deal. A strong personal brand can make you indispensable to your clients, partners, and even your own organization.

## WHY PERSONAL BRANDING MATTERS IN SALES

**Builds Trust and Credibility:** Salespeople with strong personal brands are seen as more trustworthy and credible by prospects and clients. When people see that you consistently deliver value, offer insights, and maintain a positive reputation, they're more likely to trust you with their business. Your personal brand becomes a bridge to stronger client relationships.

**Differentiates You From Competitors:** In a crowded market, products and services can start to feel similar to customers. What makes the difference? You do. Your unique personal brand can be the deciding factor that makes a client choose you over your competitors. It's your personal touch, your expertise, and your way of connecting that stand out.

**Establishes You as an Expert:** Through personal branding, you position yourself as an expert in your niche. Whether it's sharing insights on social media, speaking at industry events, or writing thought-leadership articles, you create a reputation as someone who knows the industry inside out. This expertise makes people more inclined to seek your advice, view you as a thought leader, and value your opinion.

**Generates Referrals and Leads:** A well-crafted personal brand attracts both clients and opportunities. People in your network are more likely to refer you when they know what you stand for and the value you bring. It's like having a 24/7 business card circulating in the market that brings leads to you organically.

**Helps Navigate Tough Negotiations:** Clients are more likely to negotiate with you favorably if they respect your brand and reputation. A well-established personal brand conveys that you are a person of integrity who delivers on promises and is worth the investment. This reputation makes negotiations smoother and more productive.

**Creates Impact Like a Top Lawyer:** Think of a courtroom setting. Imagine a lawyer who has handled high-profile cases successfully. The moment someone hears about that lawyer appearing in court, there's a buzz—"Oh, him!" That's the kind of impact your personal brand should create in sales. When prospects and clients hear that *you* are handling the deal, they should feel reassured and confident that they are in capable hands.

**Makes You Indispensable:** A strong personal brand can make you indispensable—not just to your clients, but also to your own organization. You want your company to think, "We need him there," and for clients to say, "I need him on this project." When your expertise is trusted, your presence becomes more than just a name on an email—it's a crucial part of their decision-making process.

**Helps Gain Mass Appeal:** Your personal brand should give you a reputation that precedes you. Just like that of the best lawyer in court, your name should carry weight. Clients and prospects should recognize you, admire your expertise, and follow your advice. Personal branding helps you establish a "mass appeal" that amplifies your influence in the market.

## HOW TO USE YOUR PERSONAL BRAND

**Stay Grounded—Branding Is Not Boasting:** Personal branding should never be confused with boasting. The best salespeople are those who let their actions speak louder than their words. Fame and recognition will come naturally if your work, pitch, and content are impactful. Humility is key—stay grounded, and your brand will speak for itself.

**Be the Expert Advisor:** Your personal brand should reflect that you are not just a salesperson, but a trusted advisor. This advice goes beyond selling—it's about being someone to whom prospects, clients, and even colleagues turn for insight and guidance. They should feel they "need you" because you offer more than a product; you offer expertise and value that others can't match.

**Maintain a Strong Social Profile:** In today's digital age, your social media presence plays a significant role in your personal branding. Be a sales professional that others aspire to be, someone they admire and follow. Share insights, engage with industry trends, and continuously build your network. Your social media should reinforce the brand you've built in the real world.

## HOW TO BUILD A POWERFUL PERSONAL BRAND

**Define Your Unique Value Proposition:** Just as you differentiate products, you need to define what makes you unique. What do you stand for? What are your strengths? What can clients expect from you that they won't get from someone else? Your value proposition should be clear in every interaction—whether it is online, through email, or in face-to-face meetings.

**Be Consistent Across Channels:** Your personal brand should be consistent on every platform—whether it is LinkedIn, X/

Twitter, your company website, or in person. The tone, values, and personality you convey should remain the same, reinforcing a strong and reliable image. This consistency creates a cohesive brand that others can trust.

**Share Valuable Content:** The more value you provide, the stronger your brand becomes. Share insights, trends, and knowledge related to your field. Providing entails more than promoting your product. You need to offer solutions to industry problems, share case studies, or provide actionable advice. Being a resource makes you invaluable.

**Network Intentionally:** Building a personal brand also means building connections. Attend events, join industry groups, and network with peers and clients. Being active in the community builds visibility and trust, allowing you to expand your brand's reach and influence.

**Be Authentic and Genuine:** The foundation of a strong personal brand is authenticity. Clients can spot insincerity, and if your brand is built on a façade, it won't last long. Be genuine in your interactions, both online and offline. Authenticity breeds trust, and trust builds long-term relationships.

## EXERCISE: BUILDING YOUR PERSONAL BRAND IN SALES

Here's an actionable exercise to help you start building your personal brand:

- **List Your Strengths and Values:** Write down the qualities that make you a strong salesperson. Is it your ability to build relationships? Your expertise in a specific industry? Your approach to solving customer problems?
- **Identify Your Target Audience:** Whom are you trying to reach with your personal brand? Your existing clients? Potential leads? Your colleagues in the industry?
- **Create Your Elevator Pitch:** Craft a short, compelling statement that captures your personal brand. This pitch should include who you are, what you do, and the value you bring. Make sure it aligns with your values and strengths.
- **Optimize Your LinkedIn Profile:** Update your LinkedIn profile to reflect your personal brand. Make sure your bio, job descriptions, and posts align with the image you want to project.
- **Engage With Your Network:** Start posting valuable content, commenting on industry discussions, and participating in relevant groups. The more active and visible you are, the stronger your brand will become.

This comprehensive chapter emphasizes how essential personal branding is for a successful sales career. By following these steps, every salesperson can build a personal brand that sets them apart from the competition, earns trust, and generates more opportunities.

# 15

# How to Ensure You Always Stand Out in Sales

"Prospects can tell when you're being authentic versus when you're just trying to make a sale."

Ensuring that you **always stand out** in sales requires a combination of mindset, skills, and habits that continually set you apart from the competition. Here are key strategies to help you consistently differentiate yourself:

### 1. Master the Art of Listening

Most salespeople are eager to talk, pitch, and present. The **best salespeople** stand out by being great listeners. When you actively listen, you can uncover the prospect's pain points, desires, and concerns in ways that others might miss. Listening carefully allows you to tailor your message precisely, which makes a lasting impression.

### 2. Personalize Every Interaction

Clients and prospects remember those who **personalize** their communication. Whether it's remembering a detail from a previous conversation or adjusting your approach to suit their specific situation, personalization shows that you care about them as individuals. This small touch often makes you memorable because most salespeople use a one-size-fits-all approach.

### 3. Stay Proactive, Not Reactive

Don't wait for the prospect to come to you with questions or concerns—anticipate their needs. Being proactive means consistently following up, offering valuable information before they ask for it, and staying ahead of their concerns. It's about guiding the process rather than waiting for it to unfold. **Proactivity** sets you apart because it shows you're one step ahead of the competition.

### 4. Build a Reputation as a Problem Solver

Clients value salespeople who position themselves as **problem solvers**, not just product pushers. Always approach conversations with the mindset of helping the client win. Offer insights, suggest creative solutions, or provide guidance even when it is not directly related to the sale. It helps you to be seen a trusted advisor and makes you stand out.

### 5. Show Confidence, Not Arrogance

Confidence sells, but arrogance turns people away. The key is to approach every conversation with the **confidence** that you can provide real value, without coming across as pushy or egotistical. Confidence assures the prospect that you know your product and understand their needs, while humility builds trust.

### 6. Offer Unique Insights and Value

You stand out when you offer **unique insights** that your competitors aren't providing. To do so means staying informed about your industry, understanding the prospect's market, and delivering fresh perspectives that they might not have considered. The more you can educate the prospect and position yourself as a resource, the more they will remember you and rely on you.

### 7. Be Consistent in Communication

Consistency is a simple yet powerful tool to ensure you stand out. Regular, meaningful communication keeps you at the top of the prospect's mind. Going beyond follow-ups, this communication involves consistently providing value, whether by sharing case studies, offering solutions, or simply checking in. Many salespeople lose momentum, but consistency makes you dependable and trustworthy.

### 8. Focus on Building Long-Term Relationships, Not Just Closing the Deal

Sales isn't just about the current transaction—it is about building **relationships** that last. When you focus on the long-term relationship rather than just closing the deal, you create loyalty and trust. Prospects and clients will come back to you because they know you're in it for the long haul, not just the quick win.

### 9. Be Authentic and Sincere

Prospects can tell when you're being authentic versus when you're just trying to make a sale. **Authenticity** means being genuine in your approach—whether you're sharing good news or difficult truths. When you're sincere, clients feel that they can trust you, and that trust will set you apart from competitors who may only care about achieving their numbers.

### 10. Always Keep Learning and Evolving

The best salespeople never stop learning. They're always adapting to new trends, learning from every interaction, and improving their skills. To ensure you always stand out, you need to **keep evolving**—by improving your product knowledge, honing your communication skills, and staying updated on the latest market shifts.

#### CLOSING THOUGHT

Standing out isn't about being the loudest or the flashiest—it is about consistently adding **real value**. Whether it is through listening, personalization, problem-solving, or being proactive, your goal is to make every interaction with the prospect meaningful. When you combine these qualities with confidence, authenticity, and a constant drive to improve, you'll not only stand out—you'll also stay ahead of the competition every time.

# 16

# What Is an Ideal Organization for Salespeople?

"Sales success isn't just about the salesperson—it is about the system that supports them."

The environment in which a salesperson operates is critical to their success. While sales is often viewed as an individual pursuit, even the most talented salespeople can struggle if their organization doesn't have the right **system**, **culture**, and **support** in place. A company that fails to provide these elements can waste the potential of its sales team. So, what is an ideal organization for a salesperson to thrive?

### 1. A Well-Defined Sales Process

An ideal organization provides a **clear, structured sales process** that guides the salesperson at every stage, from lead generation to closing deals. Having a framework in place ensures that no steps are missed and that salespeople have the resources they need to succeed. Without this clear process, a salesperson is left to navigate their way through the chaos, often resulting in missed opportunities and frustration.

Why it matters:

A solid process provides consistency, reduces ambiguity, and enables better performance tracking. It helps salespeople focus on **selling**, not on figuring out what to do next.

### 2. Access to the Right Tools and Technology

In today's sales environment, technology plays a huge role in success. The ideal organization equips its sales team with **modern tools**, such as CRM systems, analytics platforms, automation tools, and communication technologies. These tools help salespeople manage their pipeline, track customer interactions, and analyze their performance.

Why it matters:

Without the right tools, salespeople end up spending too much time on administrative tasks, manual data entry, or chasing information. These tasks take away from their actual selling time. The best organizations understand that technology can **enhance productivity** and improve the overall sales experience for both the salesperson and the client.

### 3. A Strong Culture of Collaboration

Sales is often seen as a competitive field, but the best organizations foster a **culture of collaboration**. In an ideal sales environment, the marketing, product, support, and leadership teams work in close alignment with sales. Information flows freely between departments, and everyone works together toward a common goal.

Why it matters:

When departments operate in silos, salespeople are left in the dark. They don't have access to the latest product updates, marketing campaigns, or support issues that could affect their client conversations. In a collaborative environment, salespeople feel supported and informed, which helps them position themselves more effectively with prospects.

### 4. Continuous Learning and Development

Sales is constantly evolving, and organizations that invest in **ongoing training** and development for their sales teams create an environment where their people can thrive. An ideal organization offers coaching, mentorship, and access to resources that help salespeople refine their skills, stay up to date with industry trends, and grow both personally and professionally.

Why it matters:

A salesperson who isn't growing is stagnating. Without continuous development, even top performers can plateau. Organizations that prioritize learning empower their teams to stay sharp, adapt to changes in the market, and stay motivated.

### 5. Recognition and Incentives That Reflect Performance

Salespeople are typically motivated by achievement, and organizations that recognize their accomplishments keep morale high. The ideal company has **incentive structures** in place that reward performance—not just when quotas are achieved, but also to reward behaviors that contribute to long-term success, like building client relationships or bringing in strategic accounts.

Why it matters:

Without proper recognition, even the best salespeople can feel undervalued. This feeling can lead to frustration, burnout, and disengagement. Incentives aligned with both short-term and long-term goals help to drive consistent performance and keep the team motivated.

### 6. Leadership That Empowers, but Does Not Micromanage

An ideal organization for a salesperson has **empowering leadership** that offers guidance and support without micromanaging. Salespeople need the freedom to own their relationships, manage their pipeline, and drive results. Micromanagement can kill creativity, hinder initiative, and lead to frustration.

Why it matters:

Empowering leadership builds trust and allows salespeople to take ownership of their work. When sales leaders offer autonomy while being available for support, it creates a culture of accountability and growth. Micromanagement, on the other hand, stifles innovation and reduces motivation.

## 7. Clear Goals and Expectations

In an ideal sales organization, goals and expectations are clearly defined. This clarity means setting realistic targets, outlining the path to success, and providing feedback along the way. Salespeople need to understand what is expected of them, how they're being measured, and how they can achieve their goals.

Why it matters:

Unclear goals lead to confusion, and without clear expectations, salespeople can feel lost. Organizations that provide **clarity** give their teams the direction they need to stay focused, perform well, and avoid burnout.

## 8. A Culture That Encourages Honesty and Transparency

An ideal organization fosters a culture where salespeople can be **honest** about their challenges without fear of retribution. Salespeople should feel comfortable saying, "I missed a follow-up," "I forgot to call," or "The deal will take longer than expected." In many sales environments, pressure forces salespeople to give unrealistic projections, tell small lies, or hide mistakes just to survive.

Why it matters:

This lack of transparency can **diminish the predictability of sales revenue** and lead to inaccurate forecasts. A culture of honesty ensures that sales leaders have realistic insights into the pipeline and can make informed decisions. By allowing salespeople to speak openly, companies maintain a **healthy sales environment** that values truth over short-term wins.

### 9. A Culture of Trust and Integrity

Salespeople need to know that their organization operates with **integrity**. An ideal company fosters a culture where ethical behavior is valued and trust is built with clients. Salespeople should never feel pressured to cut corners or over-promise just to achieve targets. A culture that prioritizes long-term relationships over short-term gains builds trust internally and externally.

Why it matters:

Salespeople who are forced to operate in a high-pressure, ethically questionable environment tend to experience burnout, dissatisfaction, and client mistrust. A culture of integrity, on the other hand, empowers salespeople to do their best work while building trust with clients.

### 10. Supportive Environment for Failure and Experimentation

In sales, **not every deal will close**. The ideal organization understands this truth and creates an environment where failure is seen as part of the learning process. Salespeople need to feel safe to experiment, try new approaches, and take risks without fear of punishment.

Why it matters:

A culture that punishes failure can create fear, stifling innovation and creativity. When organizations embrace failure as a learning opportunity, salespeople feel empowered to take calculated risks and improve their performance.

## CLOSING THOUGHT

A strong system drives sales success. An ideal organization provides its salespeople with the right **structure, culture, and support** to thrive. Without this environment, even the most talented salespeople can find themselves struggling to reach their potential. From offering the right tools and technology to fostering collaboration, continuous learning, and honest communication, organizations that focus on building a strong sales environment empower their teams to achieve great things.

The truth is that a great salesperson in a bad system can only go so far. But a great salesperson in the right system will thrive, innovate, and consistently deliver results.

# 17

# Procurement vs. the Salesperson: The Ultimate Negotiation Clash

"It's not just about the price; it's about winning the value battle."

In sales, one team you'll often face in a **strategic battle** is the **procurement or prospects' purchase team**. While your goal is to maintain margins and close the deal, the procurement team has a different mission: securing the best price, often measured by how much the team can "save" for the company. The procurement team's key performance indicators (KPIs) are tied to how much **discount** they can squeeze from vendors. On the other hand, your mission is to maximize the value of the deal. So, how do you navigate this tug-of-war and come out on top?

The key to winning this battle lies in understanding the team's tactics, preparing during the **brainstorming stage (see Chapter**

**6: Brainstorming for Pricing**), and positioning yourself to hold firm during negotiations without compromising too much. Let's dive into how you can maintain a **good relationship** with this team while still achieving **your goals**.

### 1. The Procurement Team's Favorite Line: "Your Pricing Is Too High"

If you've ever negotiated with this team, you've likely heard this sentence: "Your pricing is too high." The procurement team will often push back with this sentence, even if your price is within reason. Sometimes, they'll even claim your price is **above their target pricing**. However, would they ever say, "Your price is actually below our budget, so here's some more money?" Of course not.

This is a **common tactic**. The team will play up the price to push for discounts, and as we discussed in **Chapter 6** (**Brainstorming for Pricing**), you need to be prepared for this eventuality. When brainstorming the price, consider the **maximum discount** you can offer, but never assume you will get away without being challenged on the number you initially present. Procurement teams are skilled at negotiating down, but you should already have your **minimum acceptable price** in mind.

### 2. Prepare During the Pricing Brainstorming

During the pricing **brainstorming session** (as discussed in Chapter 6), you'll need to account for the inevitable pressure from the procurement team. When you quote your price, keep in mind that they will **always ask for more discounts**—this is where the battle begins. You must anticipate this pushback and prepare how much **leeway** you're willing to give. Remember, the goal is to hold the line as much as possible without losing the deal.

You can use **strategic discounts** as leverage. For example, offer a discount only if the customer agrees to longer contract terms or increases the volume of the order. By doing this, you maintain the value of the deal while giving procurement something they can report as a win.

### 3. Make Procurement Work for You by Creating Urgency

A great tactic to motivate the procurement team is by **creating a sense of urgency**. One way is to offer a **time-sensitive discount**. For example, if the team issues the purchase order (PO) by a specific date, they can get a certain discount. This urgency pushes procurement to act quickly, especially when they're trying to show savings on a tight timeline. By offering a **deadline-driven incentive**, you shift the power back to yourself, allowing you to maintain control of the negotiation while still offering value.

**Why it works:** Procurement teams have targets to meet, and a time-sensitive discount creates a win-win situation. They get to report immediate savings, and you secure the deal faster without dragging out the negotiation process.

### 4. Know the Market: Confidently Challenge False Claims

One of the most valuable assets in any sales negotiation is **market knowledge**. When the procurement team claims that your price is higher than that of your competitors, it is often a tactic to squeeze more out of the deal. But if you have a **strong understanding of your competitors' pricing**, you can confidently **challenge those claims**.

**Why it matters:** If you know your competitors' pricing, and the procurement team says your price is too high, you can push back and say, "That's not true. We're in the market, and we understand the prices that others quote." This level of confidence shows the team that you're not just relying on your own solution—you're also well-informed about what's happening in the industry. This kind of knowledge, combined with strong presence of mind, can turn the negotiation in your favor.

### 5. Emphasize Value Over Price

When the team asks for discounts or claims your price is too high, it is tempting to lower your number to get closer to their "target." However, doing so could erode your margins and send the message that the value of your product isn't as strong as you initially stated. Instead, **defend your value**.

Use the strategies from **Chapter 4 (Tailoring the Presentation)** to present the value of your solution. If you've built a strong case for how your solution solves the client's problems, then your pricing is **justified**. Keep emphasizing the **long-term benefits** and ROI. This perspective shifts the conversation from a battle over price to a discussion about **overall value**.

### 6. Use Tactical Discounts: Packages, Not Percentages

The trick is to make sure that any discount that you offer feels earned. Instead of giving a flat percentage discount, offer **packages** that give the procurement team something extra while maintaining the integrity of your pricing. For example, if the team is pushing for a 15% discount, instead of immediately lowering the price, offer a **smaller discount** (say 5%) and add in something of value, like extended warranties, additional support, or future discounts on other products.

This way, the procurement team still feels like they've won something, but you haven't lost **significant margin**. Always present your discounts as part of a bigger **package**, which ties back to your pricing strategy.

### 7. Build Rapport—It's Not Just Business

One often-overlooked aspect of dealing with procurement is the importance of **building rapport**. Procurement professionals are people too, and they value relationships. Show that you're willing to work with them, listen to their concerns, and find creative solutions that meet both parties' needs.

In **Chapter 7 (Building Relationships for Long-Term Success)**, we explored the power of building long-term connections. The same principles apply to the procurement team too. By maintaining a strong relationship, you create trust, making future negotiations smoother.

## CASE STUDY: NAVIGATING A TOUGH PROCUREMENT NEGOTIATION

### The Situation:

In one of my key deals, I was negotiating with a major corporate client who was keen on our **Facilities Management System**. Everything was looking promising until the procurement team stepped in, demanding a **20% discount** and comparing our price with a lower quote from a competitor.

### The Challenge:

The team was laser-focused on reducing the price. They claimed that our competitor was offering similar features at a lower cost. I knew we couldn't match their price without slashing our margins significantly, but I also didn't want to lose the deal.

### The Approach:

Instead of jumping into discount negotiations, I spent time positioning our product's **unique value**. I emphasized that while the competitor's product was cheaper, it lacked critical features that were essential for the long-term success of their operations. Additionally, I framed our pricing as an **investment** rather than a cost.

Next, I used a **tactical discount strategy**: I offered a **5% discount**, but only if they agreed to a **three-year contract** and added an **additional service module**. I also sweetened the deal by offering a **price freeze** for future purchases in the next two years.

### The Result:

The procurement team accepted the deal with the smaller discount. They were able to report savings back to their company, and I managed to secure a long-term, high-value contract without severely compromising our margins. This approach helped me maintain a **strong relationship** with the procurement team and opened the door for future business.

### CLOSING THOUGHT

Outplay procurement by playing smart. Procurement teams will always push back on price—that's their job. But your job is to **defend your value**, understand their tactics, and approach the negotiation strategically. By preparing during the **pricing brainstorming phase (Chapter 6)**, positioning your solution as offering high value (Chapter 4), and building rapport (Chapter 7), you'll be able to win over procurement without giving away too much.

The goal isn't just to win the deal—it is to win it **on your terms**.

# 18

# Turning the Tables: Keeping Procurement on the Back Foot Without Losing the Deal

"In sales, silence, timing, and staying calm can be louder than a thousand discounts."

During the peak of the COVID-19 pandemic, a leading Indian bank urgently needed a software solution to streamline its return-to-office plan. The bank's facilities were closed, and the team wanted our workplace management software implemented swiftly before resuming operations. For someone working in software sales, this opportunity was a big one—especially at a time when most deals were drying up.

The inquiry came from the bank's assistant vice president (AVP) – IT, and over the next few days, I engaged with the senior vice president (SVP) as well, who was actively involved in demos, requirement discussions, and finalization. Given the urgency and the reputation of the client, I worked proactively and quoted 20% lower than our standard rates to make the offer compelling while still protecting our margins.

The team appreciated the product, told me openly that our pricing was reasonable, and assured me that final procurement discussions were just a formality. However, what seemed like a smooth final step turned into an unexpected challenge.

## THE PROCUREMENT SURPRISE

Forty-eight days after our initial interaction, I received an invite for a final negotiation call with the procurement team. As always, I did my homework. I looked up all participants. One name stood out—a mid-level procurement manager who had joined recently. I had never interacted with him before.

As the meeting began, he introduced himself and then asked the usual: company profile, product history, years in business, and so on. I patiently explained. Then came the bombshell.

"This is your own product, right? So, by now, you must have recovered all of your development cost," remarked the manager. "We are a reputed bank. You should feel privileged to work with us. I suggest you offer your software license to us for free and charge us only for implementation and customization."

The software license was the largest component in our quote.

### Staying Calm, Striking Back

Rather than getting defensive, I took a breath and calmly asked, "I see that you use SAP as your enterprise resource planning (ERP) system. You also have a requirement to integrate our software with SAP. Can I ask: Did SAP give its software to you for free?"

There was a pause. A moment of silence.

He had no answer.

Just then, I received a WhatsApp message from the SVP who was silently on the call.

*"Good going bro..."*

That single message gave me all the confidence I needed.

The procurement officer, trying to save face, replied, "If you can't give it for free, we can't move forward."

I responded without hesitation, "That's absolutely fine. Let's close the call. I'll leave the decision to your team."

### The Power of Walking Away

Sensing the momentum shift, the SVP stepped in—partially to support the procurement team.

"So, Subhash, are you saying you don't want a reputed client like us?"

I calmly replied, "If a client evaluates a product thoroughly for more than 40 days and then asks for it for free, it shows a lack of seriousness. With due respect, it doesn't matter how reputed a brand is if the product is not valued. It also wastes your time—you'll need to start again, evaluate other products, ensure compatibility, and again negotiate."

Then came the twist.

The procurement officer said, "Alright. I see you've quoted for 6 offices. Make it 15 offices—for the same cost."

I knew he just wanted something to show for his effort. It wasn't a big ask technically—it just meant enabling a few more office locations. I agreed immediately.

The SVP jumped in again, "But we don't need 15 offices."

The procurement officer replied, "Maybe not now, but it'll help in the future."

That was it. No discount. No compromise on value. Just smart positioning. The PO was issued shortly after.

### CLOSING THOUGHT

**Homework matters.** Knowing whom you're going to face and being mentally prepared makes all the difference.

**Stay calm when challenged.** I didn't react—I responded.

**Walk away if needed.** That's the ultimate negotiation power.

**Don't get provoked by "brand pressure."** Whether it's a big bank or a global firm, value your product.

**Give room to procurement to "win" something.** The additional office count helped the manager feel satisfied.

**Earn trust from decision-makers.** The SVP's support came because of the rapport and transparency I built from the first day.

# 19

# Understanding People in Sales: Recognizing Buying Signals and Navigating Price-Cut Requests

"Each buyer is different, and understanding their motivations and buying signals is the key to closing deals and handling objections effectively."

In sales, your success depends on your ability to read and respond to people. Each buyer is different, and understanding their motivations and buying signals is the key to closing deals and handling objections effectively. Some buyers will push for a price reduction as a negotiation tactic, while others may genuinely be constrained by their budget. Recognizing these differences allows you to adjust your approach, turning price objections into opportunities.

The **SWAG formula—Study, Watch, Analyze**, and **Guide**—provides a structured way to navigate buyer types, their signals, and their price objections.

## THE SWAG FORMULA IN ACTION

### S: Study the Buyer

The first step is to study the buyer's motivations and decision-making style. Are they driven by **price**, **value**, or **relationships**? Different buyer types will signal different priorities, and understanding whom you're dealing with will help you approach the negotiation with the right mindset.

### W: Watch for Buying Signals

Once you've studied the buyer, it's time to watch for their specific buying signals. These signals show where the buyer is in their decision-making process. For instance, a buyer may ask for a detailed breakdown of the pricing structure, or they may request for another meeting to discuss contract details. Recognizing these signals helps you stay on top of their concerns and adjust your strategy accordingly.

### A: Analyze the Motivation Behind Price Requests

When a buyer asks for a discount, it's important to analyze their reasons for doing so. Are they working within a limited budget, or are they testing your flexibility? The reason behind the request determines how you should respond—whether to offer a **payment plan** or a **value package**, or to hold firm.

### G: Guide the Conversation to Win

Once you've studied, watched, and analyzed the buyer's behavior, the next step is to guide the conversation toward a win-win outcome. Whether it is offering a **small discount with conditions**, providing extra services to justify the price, or helping them see the long-term benefits, guiding the conversation ensures that the buyer feels they're getting value while you maintain your margins.

## DIFFERENT TYPES OF BUYERS AND THEIR BUYING SIGNALS

### 1. The Bargain Hunter: Focused on Price

Bargain hunters are focused on the deal—they want to feel like they've won by securing the best price. They'll often start negotiating right away and will compare your offer to those of your competitors.

**Buying Signals**: Constant pushback on price, requests for competitor pricing

**SWAG Application**: Study their price-focused mindset, watch for signals of dissatisfaction with value, and guide the conversation by adding value instead of lowering the price outright.

### 2. The Indecisive Buyer: Needs Assurance

These buyers are hesitant, unsure of whether they're making the right decision. They'll often stall, asking for more information or time.

**Buying Signals**: Repeated requests for product details, delays in decision-making

**SWAG Application**: Watch for hesitation, analyze their need for confidence, and guide them with case studies, guarantees, or testimonials to build their trust in your solution.

### 3. The Budget-Conscious Buyer: Limited by Funds

Genuinely constrained by budget, these buyers need flexibility to move forward.

**Buying Signals**: Honest discussion about financial limitations, disappointment with pricing

**SWAG Application**: Study their financial constraints, analyze how flexible they can be, and guide them by offering scaled-down options or extended payment terms without dropping the price significantly.

### 4. The Analytical Buyer: Data-Driven Decision-Maker

These buyers base their decisions on data and logic. They need numbers to back up your claims and will compare every aspect of your offer to alternatives.

**Buying Signals**: Detailed questions, requests for technical specs and cost breakdowns

**SWAG Application**: Analyze their need for facts and figures, and guide the conversation with detailed data and case studies that emphasize ROI.

### 5. The Emotional Buyer: Relationship-Focused

This buyer prioritizes trust and relationships. They value the connection they have with you and may ask for a discount out of loyalty.

**Buying Signals**: Focus on past interactions, requests for a "special" deal based on your relationship

**SWAG Application**: Study their reliance on relationships, and guide the conversation by offering loyalty perks or reinforcing the long-term partnership rather than cutting the price.

## CASE STUDY: HANDLING A BARGAIN-HUNTER BUYER

### The Situation:

A prospective client from a large enterprise approached us for our **Facilities Management System**. From the start, it was clear that they were price-focused, continuously comparing our solution to cheaper competitors and pushing for a large discount.

### The Challenge:

The client asked for a **25% discount**, claiming that another vendor had offered them a similar product at a much lower price. However, I knew that our system had features that the competitor didn't offer, and cutting prices by that much would reduce our margins significantly.

### The SWAG Application:

**Study**: I recognized early on that this client was a classic **bargain hunter**, motivated primarily by getting the best deal possible. They weren't concerned about value, just price.

**Watch**: I noticed their constant requests for competitor pricing, along with comments like, "Can you match this price?" This attitude indicated that price was their main concern, not the product's benefits.

**Analyze**: I knew that they were using the competitor's pricing as a negotiation tactic, but I also understood that they valued a solid, long-term solution. The real issue wasn't the price—it was proving the **value**.

**Guide**: Rather than dropping our price immediately, I took control of the conversation by offering a **small discount**, tied to a longer contract period and additional services that the competitor couldn't match. I also emphasized the long-term savings and superior ROI of our system, guiding the buyer to see that paying a bit more up front would save them money in the long run.

### The Result:

The client accepted the smaller discount and signed a three-year contract. They were able to report cost savings to their management, and we retained our margins while securing a long-term relationship. By applying the SWAG formula, I navigated the price objection and won the deal on terms that worked for both sides.

### CLOSING THOUGHT

Mastering sales is about more than just presenting your product. It's about understanding the **people** you're dealing with, recognizing their **buying signals**, and adapting your approach to address their concerns while still maintaining your value. By applying the **SWAG formula**, you can win over any buyer type, whether they're pushing for discounts, asking for more information, or hesitating on a decision. Sales is about **relationships and strategy**, and by mastering both, you'll consistently close deals on your terms.

# 20

# How to Set Up a Fantastic Sales Process and Ensure It Drives Results and Targets

"A seamless process drives predictable success and growth—empowering your sales team to perform, not just survive."

In sales, it is not enough to have a great product or a skilled team; without a structured and repeatable process, the results are left to chance. A **systematic sales process** ensures that every member of your team knows what to do, when to do it, and how to follow through. The key is to create a **system-driven process** that drives both **targets** and **results**.

Let's break down the elements that make a sales process truly effective and discuss how it can empower the team to achieve targets consistently.

### 1. Conduct Regular Reviews to Keep Sales on Track

Regular **reviews**—whether daily, weekly, or monthly—are essential to keep the sales process on track. Reviews should be **motivational and constructive**, not an exercise in criticism.

- **Daily Reviews**: Focus on quick check-ins to ensure immediate priorities (for example, lead follow-ups or pending proposals) are being addressed.
- **Weekly Reviews**: Evaluate progress on midterm goals, such as demos completed, proposals submitted, and key client interactions.
- **Monthly Reviews**: Take a broader view of the health of the sales pipeline, performance against targets, and strategic shifts if necessary.

Why Reviews Matter:

- **Rejuvenate, Don't Demotivate**: Reviews should re-energize the team, not discourage them. Use these sessions to provide constructive feedback that helps salespeople course correct without feeling defeated.
- **Set Clear Action Points**: For every review, make sure action items are documented and tracked. Whether it is following up on leads, sending proposals on time, or scheduling client visits, there should be deadlines and accountability.

### 2. Monitor Action Points and Support Salespeople in Execution

A well-defined process involves tracking the following specific **action points** that salespeople must execute:

- **Following up on leads**: Ensure that no lead goes cold from neglect.
- **Sending proposals/quotations on time**: Timeliness is crucial to show professionalism and maintain momentum.
- **Scheduling meetings or trips**: In some cases, face-to-face interaction or travel may be needed to close deals.
- **Supporting sales with leadership involvement**: Managers or senior leadership should step in when higher-level involvement is necessary, such as in complex negotiations or large deals.

**Expand the List**: Customize this action list based on your team's needs. The more clarity there is, the easier it is to monitor and guide progress. Setting **specific deadlines** ensures that tasks are completed in a timely manner, preventing bottlenecks in the sales cycle.

### 3. Set Activity-Based Targets Instead of Purely Sales Targets

While achieving sales targets is critical for growth, activity-based targets create a strong foundation for those numbers. Activity-based targets focus on the actions that **lead to closing deals**, not just the deal itself.

Why Activity Targets Work:

- **Focus on Actions That Drive Results**: By emphasizing activities such as calls made, demos conducted, or proposals sent, salespeople stay **engaged** and **consistent** in their efforts. These actions naturally lead to achieving **sales numbers.**
- **Sales Targets Alone Create Pressure**: Focusing solely on the end goal (sales numbers) can create immense pressure, especially if deals fall through at the last minute. Activity-based targets ensure progress is being made, even if some deals take longer to close.

**Examples of activity targets** include the number of **leads/inquiries** handled per week, **presentations/demos** scheduled, and **proposals/quotations** submitted. Tracking these activities presents a clearer picture of the efforts being put in and the effectiveness of those efforts.

### 4. Make Salespeople Accountable for Their Own Progress

A fantastic process also empowers the sales team to take ownership of their progress. Through regular reviews and the use of **activity reports**, salespeople can see for themselves where they stand in terms of **actual vs. achieved**.

**Self-Evaluation**: By maintaining an activity report, salespeople can identify gaps in their efforts and adjust their approach before it is too late. This self-accountability ensures that the **sales process** is followed without constant supervision and drives consistent results.

### 5. Ensure the Process Drives the System, Not the Individual

A process-oriented approach means that the sales team is **guided by the system**, not by individual whims or habits. The system ensures consistency, quality, and reliability in every sales interaction.

**Why It Matters**: If the process is strong, results will follow, no matter who is executing it. A strong process reduces the risk of **overdependence on star performers** and ensures that the entire team contributes to the success of the organization.

**Future-Proofing**: When they follow a system, your salespeople will thank you not only while they're with your company but also as they move through their careers. They'll carry forward the discipline and structure that helped them succeed under your leadership.

### 6. Set Up a Process-Oriented Culture That Makes a Lasting Impact

Creating a **process-oriented culture** in your sales team ensures that the organization remains focused on the system rather than individual-driven performance. This culture becomes ingrained in how the team operates, giving clarity and purpose to their work.

When speaking with peers from other organizations, many sales leaders report issues caused by a lack of process and frequent changes in direction. This is a **dangerous situation**—teams become **disoriented**, and motivation drops. A stable, well-defined process mitigates this risk by giving the team a clear path forward, no matter the external challenges.

### 7. Activity-Based Targets Will Seamlessly Lead to Sales Targets

While **sales targets** (the numbers) are essential to drive growth, activity-based targets keep the team focused on what really drives those numbers. By setting clear activity targets, your team can reach the numbers without feeling **overwhelmed** or unsure of their progress.

- **Sales Targets Without Process = Chaos**: If the team is only chasing a number, the focus may shift to **short-term gains** and **cutting corners** to hit targets, ultimately damaging long-term success.
- **Activity Targets Create Momentum**: When you know how many calls, demos, or proposals are being handled, the numbers start to add up. Consistent activities build toward **consistent results**.

## MAINTAINING PROFESSIONAL HYGIENE AND BEING A DISCIPLINED SALESPERSON

A **disciplined salesperson** goes beyond following a process—they maintain **professional hygiene** by sticking to ethical, punctual, and systematic sales behaviors.

### 1. Punctuality and Commitment

A disciplined salesperson respects deadlines and follows through on promises. Whether it's sending a proposal, scheduling a follow-up, or attending a meeting, punctuality demonstrates **reliability** and builds **trust**.

### 2. Keeping the CRM Clean and Up-to-Date

Maintaining clean and accurate data is part of professional hygiene. Keeping the **CRM updated** ensures that no lead is left unattended and provides management with **real-time insights**.

### 3. Organized Follow-Ups

Following up is an essential discipline. Keep track of every prospect and follow up at the right moments. Avoid pushy follow-ups and instead maintain a **personalized, meaningful connection** with the client.

### 4. Ethical Sales Practices

Always stay ethical in your sales approach. Don't over-promise or mislead clients just to close a deal. Maintain a balance between being persuasive and being **transparent** about what your product can or cannot do.

### CLOSING THOUGHT

A process-driven approach is important for sales success. The real magic happens when salespeople are not left guessing about how to achieve their targets. Instead, a **process-driven approach** ensures that daily actions align with long-term goals. It creates **predictable results** and an **engaged team** that feels confident and equipped to achieve their targets.

# 21

# Understanding Customer Persona and Selling

"Selling to everyone is like selling to no one. Understand the person's needs, and the deal is halfway done."

When it comes to sales, a one-size-fits-all approach can be detrimental. Every prospect within an organization—be it the manager, CEO, CFO, or IT/InfoSec officer—has different pain points, priorities, and motivations. Understanding these personas is essential for a successful pitch. Customizing your approach for each audience based on their specific needs can elevate your effectiveness as a salesperson.

## THE IMPORTANCE OF TAILORING YOUR PITCH TO DIFFERENT PERSONAS

### Different Roles, Different Pain Points

A manager might be more focused on daily operational efficiency, while the CEO is looking at strategic, long-term growth. The

CFO is concerned with the financial impact, and the IT/InfoSec officer wants to ensure security and compliance. When you pitch the same solution to all these personas without customization, you're missing the mark.

- **Managers** are often focused on performance metrics, employee productivity, and operational bottlenecks
- **CEOs** are concerned about business scalability, revenue growth, maintaining a competitive edge, and innovation.
- **CFOs** focus on ROI, total cost of ownership (TCO), budget constraints, and financial risk.
- **IT/InfoSec officers** focus on data security, regulatory compliance, systems integration, and potential technology risks.

## WHY A GENERIC PITCH DOESN'T WORK

Even if you've prepared a presentation tailored to a specific company, presenting the same material to various decision-makers without altering it can be counterproductive. Each role within an organization has unique goals, and your message must resonate with those goals.

For example, pitching a tech-heavy solution to a CFO without focusing on the financial benefits might cause them to lose interest. Similarly, instead of talking too much about the budget to an IT head, you could use the opportunity to address their need for technical precision and security.

## UNDERSTANDING THE AUDIENCE'S ROLE

Sales is like offering different dishes to various customers. You wouldn't try to sell a grilled chicken platter in a region where non-vegetarian food is prohibited. Similarly, you can't pitch features and benefits irrelevant to the person's role within the company. Understanding the customer's persona helps you cater to their specific tastes and needs, making the pitch more relatable and impactful.

## CUSTOMIZING THE PITCH: ADAPTING TO DIFFERENT PERSONAS

### The Manager Persona:

For managers, the key is to focus on **efficiency, day-to-day operational improvements**, and the role of the solution in making their team's job easier. Highlight how the software will help them track metrics, streamline processes, and manage resources more effectively.

**Example Pitch**: "Our solution helps you automate your workflows, reducing time spent on manual tasks by 30%, which gives you more time to focus on high-priority initiatives and improves team efficiency."

### The CEO Persona:

CEOs are focused on the bigger picture. They want to know how the solution contributes to long-term growth, profitability, and the company's competitive edge. Show how the product can position them as leaders in their industry.

**Example Pitch**: "By implementing this software, you'll have the foundation to scale operations without increasing overhead costs, giving your company a strategic advantage in expanding market share."

### The CFO Persona:

CFOs want to understand the financial implications. They are concerned about cost-effectiveness, ROI, and risk mitigation. The key here is to provide a clear financial justification, demonstrating cost savings and increased profitability over time.

**Example Pitch**: "Our solution delivers an ROI of 200% within the first year by significantly reducing resource wastage and optimizing financial workflows, saving you [X]% annually in operational costs."

### The IT/InfoSec Persona:

For IT and InfoSec officers, the conversation should revolve around data security, systems integration, and technological reliability. They want to ensure the solution is robust, scalable, and does not introduce vulnerabilities.

**Example Pitch**: "Our software meets top-tier security standards, and it is fully compliant with General Data Protection Regulation (GDPR) and other regulatory frameworks. It integrates seamlessly with your existing systems, minimizing disruption while ensuring data integrity."

## ADAPTING THE SALES PROCESS TO CUSTOMER PERSONA

### Research and Preparation:

Before you approach any sales pitch, it's important to do your homework. Understand who will be attending the meeting, their role within the company, and the specific challenges they face. Adjust your message accordingly to speak directly to their concerns.

### Multi-Persona Presentations:

When presenting to multiple stakeholders with different personas, balance your pitch by addressing each of their concerns without diluting the message. This requires structuring your presentation with sections for ROI, operational efficiency, scalability, and security, and then pivoting based on the person's role during the conversation.

### Engage Individually if Possible:

If you have the opportunity, engage each persona separately. A one-on-one conversation allows you to dive deeper into their specific needs without the distraction of competing priorities.

### The Power of Persona-Specific Selling

Selling with the persona in mind enhances your credibility, trust, and effectiveness. Tailored communication demonstrates that you understand the prospect's business, care about their specific challenges, and are genuinely invested in helping them achieve success. This persona-driven approach also strengthens your relationship with the client, which can lead to faster deal closures and longer-term partnerships.

**CLOSING THOUGHT**

Customer personas in sales aren't just theoretical concepts—they are practical tools that help you refine your strategy, craft the right message, and address the real-world needs of each decision-maker. Personalization and preparation are crucial to stand out in today's competitive sales environment.

# 22

# Effective Partner Handling: Getting the Most out of Partners, Resellers, and System Integrators

"Partners are your extended salesforce—nurture them right, and they'll multiply your impact across markets."

In today's competitive landscape, partners—whether they are **resellers**, **system integrators**, or **channel partners**—are essential for expanding your reach and scaling your business. A partner can represent your brand, promote your solutions, and provide inroads into regions or sectors where your direct sales team might not have a presence. Managing these partnerships effectively requires a **strategic approach** that benefits both sides.

## UNDERSTANDING YOUR PARTNERS: BIG PLAYERS, NICHE OPERATORS, AND SYSTEM INTEGRATORS

Partners come in all shapes and sizes, and understanding the different types of partners you engage with is the first step toward leveraging their potential.

- **Big Companies**: Large partners often package your solution with other complementary offerings to present a complete solution to their clients. Their wide customer base and established networks can help you break into **new markets** or industries.
- **Small/Niche Companies**: These partners may be smaller in size but are often more **agile**. They can identify specific opportunities that fit perfectly with your offerings and are motivated to engage closely with you to win those deals.
- **System Integrators (SIs)**: These companies combine your product with other systems to create a tailored solution for their clients. **SIs** play a crucial role in complex projects where your solution needs to integrate with existing infrastructure or services.

**The Advantage**: One of the greatest benefits of having a partner network is the **regional footprint** it provides. If a partner has a strong presence in a particular region or sector, your solution gets attention in places where you might not have a direct presence.

## VALIDATING YOUR PARTNERS: ENSURING ALIGNMENT AND TRUST

Choosing the right partners is critical, as not every partnership will be beneficial in the long term. It's important to ensure that both your company and the partner have **shared goals and mutual interests**.

- **Validating the Partner's Fit**: Whether they approach you or you seek them out, the validation process ensures that you're both aligned. The partner should understand your **terms and conditions**, know how to represent your product truthfully, and have a good reputation in their industry.
- **Avoiding Exaggeration**: Be wary of partners who over-promise or **exaggerate** your offerings just to close a deal. This attitude can damage your reputation and result in unhappy customers. A partner that makes **fake commitments** can be a liability in the long run.
- **The Risk of Poor Partnering**: If the partner doesn't meet expectations or **goofs up**, it's not just their reputation at risk—your product or solution may also earn a bad name. **Choosing the right partners** and keeping them in check ensures that both sides benefit from the relationship.

## DRAWING THE LINE: CLEARLY DEFINING ROLES AND RESPONSIBILITIES

Clear boundaries are essential in every partnership. **Defining roles** and having a solid agreement ensures that both parties know their responsibilities, preventing confusion or disputes down the line.

- **Role Clarity**: Document the role of the partner and your own role in the engagement. This delineation eliminates any ambiguity and avoids overlap, especially when it comes to communication with the client.
- **Deal Locking**: Ensure you have a proper **deal-locking system** in place. If a partner brings a lead, that lead should be **locked under their name** in your CRM or via an official confirmation. This process prevents the risk of the client bypassing the partner and coming directly to you or another partner attempting to poach the deal.
- **The Benefit of Deal Locking**: This system encourages **professionalism** and enhances **trust**. Partners feel confident that the leads they bring in are safe under their name, leading to long-term collaboration.

## HANDLING PARTNERS TACTFULLY: BALANCING EXPECTATIONS

Partners don't get paid unless they close a deal, unlike salespeople who receive their salary every month. This unique challenge requires careful handling to keep partners motivated and engaged.

- **Managing Motivation**: Even if a partner takes several proposals from you but fails to close deals, you must handle them **tactfully**. Pressure won't help—**supporting**

**them**, keeping their spirits high, and maintaining a strong relationship are more beneficial.

- **Joint Client Meetings**: When you share commercials with a partner, it's common for them to add their margin and submit the final proposal to the client. However, being open with the partner about **winning together** builds trust. Tell them to treat you like a **buddy**, and attend client meetings together. This collaborative approach boosts their confidence and increases the chances of closing the deal.
- **Tactical Engagement**: Treat your partner as an ally, not just a channel. When partners feel supported, they're more likely to keep you as their go-to solution provider, and this relationship will strengthen your presence across regions.

## LEVERAGING PARTNERS FOR COMPETITIVE INSIGHTS AND MARKET KNOWLEDGE

Partners don't just generate leads—they can also help you understand the competitive landscape and gather **market intelligence**.

- **Understanding Competitors**: Partners often have direct insights into how your competitors operate, including their pricing strategies, weaknesses, and strengths. Use these insights to position your product better.
- **Educating Partners on Your Value**: In turn, educating your partners on how your solution **outperforms competitors** strengthens their pitch. When partners

are equipped with this knowledge, they become better advocates for your brand in the marketplace.

- **Well-Wisher Approach**: Your partner should become your strongest advocate. Even if they meet your competitors, they should say, "Hey, I have this product, and it's far better than anything else out there!" That's when you know you've built a powerful partnership.

## ENCOURAGING ENGAGEMENT AND KEEPING PARTNERS ACTIVE

Keeping partners engaged is a continuous process. It's important to build a culture of collaboration and mutual benefit.

- **Catch-Up Meetings**: Regular meetings with partners help **maintain momentum**. Discuss ongoing opportunities, new client wins, and strategies for upcoming deals.
- **Share Leads**: Don't rely solely on partners to generate leads. Share leads with them as well, creating a **two-way flow**. This boosts the partner's confidence and shows them that the partnership is truly collaborative.
- **Joint Events**: Conducting **joint events** or **webinars** with partners helps to generate visibility for both parties. It also gives the partner additional tools to pitch your solutions to their clients.
- **Stay Top of Mind**: Keep partners updated with **new launches**, **case studies**, and **client wins**. Sharing materials regularly helps them stay informed and confident in promoting your solutions. Partners should feel proud to represent your product.

- **Momentum Is Key**: With a direct lead, the salesperson handles the deal, and it's done. But when a partner gains momentum, they'll continue closing deals for you repeatedly. The more active and confident the partner becomes, the stronger the pipeline you'll have through their efforts.

### CLOSING THOUGHT

Build partnerships that thrive on collaboration and trust. A great partnership is built on **trust, mutual benefit, and continuous collaboration**. By validating your partners, maintaining clear roles, supporting them through tough times, and creating a system where both parties win, you can unlock tremendous growth. Your partners are an extension of your business, and by handling them tactfully and strategically, you can extend your reach far beyond what your internal team alone could achieve.

# 23

# The Perennial Tug of Credit: Product or Salesperson?

"Even the best dish needs a waiter to serve it right."

In almost every organization, there's an unspoken tug-of-war: **Did the product sell, or did the salesperson close the deal?** Was it the innovation, features, or market fit—or was it your relentless follow-up, pitch, and timing?

This tug is more than just semantics—it affects **internal recognition**, **motivation**, and even **career growth**. Let's explore both sides of this age-old debate and draw clear boundaries around where credit is due.

## WHEN THE PRODUCT DESERVES THE SPOTLIGHT

The product shines on its own when:

- **The brand pulls inquiries:** People reach out because they trust the product already.

- **The features solve a known problem:** The value is evident even before a deep pitch.
- **Renewals happen automatically:** The client renews licenses because the product works and delivers ROI.
- **Minimal push is needed:** There are deals where the client was already sold on the product before the salesperson joined in.

In these cases, the salesperson supports, facilitates, and ensures delivery, but the lion's share of the credit tilts toward the **product.**

## WHEN THE SALESPERSON SHOULD OWN THE WIN

There are moments when only **you** made the difference:

- **Reviving cold leads:** Deals that wouldn't have existed without your persistence
- **Handling heavy objections:** Price, features, complexity—you overcame them all
- **Switching loyalties:** When a client favored a competitor, but your pitch flipped the decision
- **Customizing proposals:** Going beyond templated decks to create something truly compelling
- **Winning trust in chaos:** Multiple stakeholders, confusion, unclear timelines—you navigated it all

In these cases, the product may be strong, but the **deal wouldn't have closed** without your skill.

## THE PERENNIAL TUG OF CREDIT

So, when do you step forward and say, *"This one was mine."*? And when do you bow gracefully and acknowledge the product's pull?

Here's the reality: **Both are needed.** However, in many companies, the salesperson doesn't get the credit they deserve—especially when the product is strong or the deal looks "easy." Similarly, salespeople should also avoid taking credit for deals where the client came pre-convinced.

The true sales pro knows **when to shine and when to support**.

### When Sales Should Take a Backseat:

- The client was already convinced before you arrived.
- The brand is the industry leader, and deals flow in naturally.
- A colleague or partner warmed the lead to the point of no resistance.
- The deal happened because of an existing mandate or compliance need.

Here, your role might be essential for smooth execution—but it's best to share the spotlight.

### When Sales Should Step Up and Claim the Credit:

- You strategized the pitch from scratch.
- You cracked the buying committee's dynamics.
- You fought delays, blockers, and tricky procurement teams.
- You converted "interest" into "urgency."

These aren't *lucky breaks*—they're earned wins.

### Why This Matters

- **For sales morale:** Credit boosts energy. Repeated neglect builds resentment.
- **For organizational clarity:** When companies understand what really works, they replicate success.
- **For cross-functional respect:** Proper credit sharing builds unity between product, sales, and delivery.

## EXERCISE: DECODING THE DEAL—WHO TRULY CLOSED IT?

This isn't about ego; it is about **clarity**.

### Step 1: Choose Three Recent Wins

Identify three deals from the past 12 months.

### Step 2: Score Yourself on the Following (Scale: 1 = Low, 5 = High)

| Factor | Description | Your Score |
|---|---|---|
| Lead Effort | Did you originate or warm up the lead? | |
| Objection Handling | Did you actively overcome roadblocks? | |
| Stakeholder Mapping | Did you identify and influence key people? | |
| Proposal Customization | Was the proposal tailored or templated? | |

| | | |
|---|---|---|
| Brand Pull | Did the brand/product bring the lead in? | |
| Urgency Creation | Did your interaction push the decision? | |
| Follow-Up Consistency | Were you actively pushing it across stages? | |
| Client Decision Trigger | Was the final decision because of your pitch? | |
| Competition Defeat | Did you defeat competitors through strategy? | |
| Execution Push | Did you accelerate timelines or unblock processes? | |

**Total Score (Per Deal):**

**40–50:** *You led this.* Take a bow.

**30–39:** *Shared win.* Team effort with your finesse.

**20–29:** *Product-led.* You facilitated an inbound pull.

**<20:** *Rethink.* Could this deal have been closed without you?

## CLOSING THOUGHT

Whether you're a waiter serving a gourmet dish or a chef preparing the menu, **both roles matter**.

Sales isn't about grabbing credit but about owning your impact with pride and humility.

Know when to **step forward**, when to **step aside**, and always **know your worth**.

# 24

# The Trump Card: Your Sales *Brahmastra*

"In sales, you don't play all your cards up front—sometimes, holding back the right move can turn the entire game in your favor."

Sales isn't just about delivering information or following a checklist of steps. It's about creating **moments of surprise**, **delight**, and **persuasion** that can make a prospect feel like they're witnessing magic. As we've discussed earlier, there's a lot of strategy in sales—from understanding the client's needs to presenting a solid value proposition—but sometimes, what seals the deal is far more subtle: the **trump card**.

Think of it as your **key weapon**, your **hidden ace**, or in more dramatic terms—your *brahmastra*. It's a piece of information or a **surprise offer** that you strategically hold back, waiting for the perfect moment to reveal it. Whether it's a **special feature**, a

**surprising discount**, or an unexpected **value proposition**, this card can be the final blow that makes your prospect surrender to your offer and **close the doors on your competitors**.

## THE THREE STAGES OF SALES MAGIC

There's a brilliant narrative structure from Christopher Nolan's *The Prestige* that mirrors this idea perfectly. In the movie, a magic trick is broken into three parts: the pledge, the turn, and the prestige. These three stages can be adapted beautifully into a **sales process** where your trump card plays the lead role.

### 1. The Pledge: Setting the Stage

In the first stage, you present the **ordinary**—what your offering, solution, or product can do. Just like a magician shows something that looks normal and unremarkable, you lay down the basic facts. This is where you establish credibility and **set expectations** for the prospect.

At this stage, you don't reveal everything. Instead, you hold back a few key elements that will later elevate the conversation.

**Example**: During a product presentation, you show the standard features of your product. The prospect is interested but not entirely convinced. You have something **extra** up your sleeve, but they don't know that yet.

### 2. The Turn: Creating Intrigue

The second stage is where the magic begins. You take something ordinary and make it **extraordinary**. In sales, this is where you start to hint at the **possibilities** and **benefits** that the client might not have fully anticipated. It is the moment you start to **turn the conversation toward closing the deal**, but the real magic hasn't happened yet.

**Example**: You explain how your solution can solve the prospect's specific problems in ways they hadn't thought of. They're interested, maybe even impressed, but they're still holding back from making a commitment.

### 3. The Prestige: Revealing the Trump Card

Now, this is where the magic happens. The **final reveal**—the **trump card** or *brahmastra* you've been holding back—is suddenly presented, and it changes everything. Whether it's a special feature that addresses a concern, a surprise discount, or a delightful commercial term they didn't expect—you deliver something that makes the prospect say, "Wow, I didn't see that coming!"

**Example**: After a long discussion and negotiation, just when the prospect thinks they've seen everything, you introduce a **special feature** or a **value-added service** that seals the deal. Maybe you've been discussing pricing and telling them that discounts aren't possible, only to suddenly offer a **special approval** that fits their budget. This unexpected move triggers a sense of **delight** and **urgency**, and before they know it, the deal is closed.

As a **funny twist**, this reminds me of how my mother handles arguments at home. She would always keep a **secret weapon**—a piece of information or a surprise detail that would instantly win the argument. No matter how much I was defending my stance, she would drop the trump card: "I know you came home drunk that day, but I didn't tell your dad." Boom! Instant victory. In sales, you need to be prepared to **pull that card** at the right time to achieve a similar effect.

## TIMING IS EVERYTHING

**Timing is crucial** when deploying your trump card. You can't reveal it too early, or you lose the impact. You can't wait too long either, or the moment passes and it loses its punch. The key is to understand **when** your prospect is close but still hesitant, and then deliver the final **wow factor** that pushes them over the line and **closes the doors on your competitors**.

## THE PSYCHOLOGY BEHIND THE TRUMP CARD

Holding back something important creates **anticipation**. By withholding certain information until the right moment, you keep the prospect intrigued and on the edge of their seat. The psychology here is simple: People love surprises, especially ones that benefit them. When you reveal something unexpected that makes their life easier or saves them money, it triggers a **positive emotional response**, making them more likely to say "yes."

### Examples of Trump Cards in Sales

- **The Surprise Feature**: Perhaps your product has a new feature that you didn't mention in the initial discussions. Save this until the negotiation stage to showcase how it offers even more value.

- **The Unexpected Discount**: If pricing has been a sticking point, and you've held firm during negotiations, the **trump card** could be a surprise discount you were authorized to offer, but only if the deal closes by a certain date.
- **Exclusive Access**: Offering **early access** to a product feature or **priority support** that wasn't initially on the table could be the final push that convinces the prospect to commit.

### CLOSING THOUGHT

Build the surprise into your sales strategy. Just like a magician knows when to hold back and when to reveal their big trick, you need to know when to play your **trump card**. This is not **deception**; it is **strategy**. Keep something in your back pocket that will leave your prospect delighted and convinced. In sales, as in magic, the final flourish is what makes the audience—or in this case, the client—**applaud** and **shut the doors on competitors**.

# 25

# Winning Against All Odds—Snatching a Deal with 85% Higher Pricing

"In sales, it is not about the lowest price; it is about building trust, delivering value, and staying calm under pressure."

## THE CHALLENGE:

While working on a high-value deal in the Middle East, I faced a significant challenge: The prospect, a newly appointed facilities manager, needed to urgently implement a facilities management software for their labor camps. However, I soon discovered that we were up against a well-established competitor that was quoting 65% lower than our price. The competitor's director of sales was handling the deal—a heavyweight in terms of experience and profile.

## THE INITIAL APPROACH:

Despite these challenges, I was determined. When the prospect requested a last-minute virtual meeting, even though my schedule was packed, I made the time. The initial conversation wasn't just about the product—it was about creating a **human connection**. We introduced ourselves, shared stories, and gradually eased into discussing the project. This casual start built a **comfortable rapport** that would later become a key factor in winning the deal.

## TAILORED PRESENTATION:

Following our initial chat, I set up a **functional demo** for him. My internal team and I prepared meticulously. We didn't just give a cookie-cutter presentation—we structured the demo to meet the **exact requirements** he outlined. By addressing his specific needs first and then showcasing additional features, we made sure he felt **in control** of the process.

## THE TURNING POINT:

It didn't take long for the prospect to share some **key insights**. He disclosed the identity of the competitor and, more importantly, mentioned that their process was slow. "You're quick; they're taking time for everything," he said. He also hinted at the budget but hadn't received the competitor's proposal yet.

I took this opportunity to submit our proposal, despite it being a holiday. My belief is that **speed** and **attentiveness** are critical in sales. I wanted to keep the momentum going.

## THE COMPETITOR'S OFFER:

Eventually, the competitor's quote came in—and it was 65% lower than ours. Surprisingly, the prospect didn't try to negotiate our price down. He liked our **product**, but more importantly, he **trusted** me. The relationship we built in those initial conversations, combined with the tailored demo, had established a level of comfort that pricing couldn't overcome.

He said, "I'm trying to close this deal quickly. Please ensure your implementation team gives us excellent support." Without hesitation, I shared my screen and showed him a **real-time WhatsApp message** from another client, praising our implementation support. The **spontaneity** of this move impressed him because I didn't take time to send an email or prepare a case study—I delivered the feedback instantly, which further **cemented trust**.

## THE COMPETITOR'S LAST-DITCH EFFORT:

Here's where it gets interesting. After the prospect informed the competitor that they had chosen us, the director of sales immediately offered an additional 20% discount, making their offer **85% lower** than ours. However, the prospect remained loyal to us. His response to the competitor's desperation was golden: "Did you know how much the vendor we finalized quoted? Did I ask for a discount?"

The competitor, sensing the deal slipping away, had their CEO call the prospect, offering personal attention and further incentives, but it was too late.

## LESSONS LEARNED:

**SEDUCE:** The trust we built early in the relationship was crucial. By understanding and empathizing with the prospect's challenges, we created a bond that couldn't be broken by a price drop.

**SNIPER:** By remaining calm and focused on the larger picture, I navigated the pressure of a pricing war and won the deal through insights, empathy, and a clear strategy.

**Trump Card:** My spontaneous sharing of real-time client feedback gave the prospect the confidence he needed to proceed. Timing is everything in sales, and having something up your sleeve to surprise and delight the prospect can close the deal.

## CLOSING THOUGHT

- **Rapport and Trust Overshadow Pricing:** Despite a massive price difference, the prospect chose us because of the trust and relationship we had built.
- **Speed and Responsiveness:** Quick responses and maintaining momentum were critical, while the competitor's delays hurt them.
- **Calm and Strategic Approach:** The competitor's aggressive discounting and follow-ups turned the prospect off, while our steady, calm approach reassured him.

- **Spontaneity and Real-Time Proof:** Showing a WhatsApp message in real time made more of an impact than any polished case study could have. Authenticity wins.

# 26

# Unlocking the Vault: Getting Key Information from Prospects

"Information isn't given; it is earned, one smart question at a time."

In sales, the real treasure lies in uncovering the details that will shape your approach—such as the prospect's **budget**, their **timeline**, and the **competitors** they are considering. This information isn't always easy to get, and it is not handed over without building trust. You have to **earn** that information through smart questioning and reading the prospect's cues.

This chapter will teach you how to **dig deep** without making your prospect feel like they're under interrogation. It's all about being **smooth**, **smart**, and just the right amount of **strategic**.

## BUILD THE BRIDGE BEFORE ASKING FOR DETAILS

Before diving into questions about budget or competitors, you need to create a **connection**. The prospect has to feel comfortable with you and **trust** you first. Without that trust, the answers you need will be harder to get.

### 1. Techniques to Build Trust

**Be a Human First**: Begin with light, human conversations. Ask about their role, their team, or what challenges they are trying to overcome. Let the product talk come naturally as you listen.

**Show That You're Listening**: Truly listen to their challenges before you start offering solutions. When a prospect feels heard, they are more likely to share valuable insights with you.

### 2. Asking About Budget: Make It Feel Like Their Idea

Budget conversations can be tricky, but if you handle them with care, you can get the details you need without making the prospect feel pressured.

**Throw in a Real Case**: You can use examples of past clients to subtly probe for budget information:

*"The recent client we won, similar to your project, had a multi-crore budget. I assume your budget would be in a similar range?"*

This approach not only helps you gauge their budget but also positions your project as **high value**.

**Offer Budget Ranges**: Instead of asking for a flat number, offer a range:

*"We typically see clients in your industry allocating between X and Y for projects of this scale. Does that sound reasonable for what you're planning?"*

**Give Them Control**: Sometimes, shifting the focus away from the exact number can make prospects more comfortable:

*"More than the budget, I think it's about finding the solution that feels right for your needs. The investment will follow naturally."*

This approach encourages prospects to share their financial range while keeping the conversation focused on value rather than cost.

### 3. Competitor Information: Gathering Without Going Hard on One

When multiple competitors are in the mix, your goal is to gather information without focusing too much on any one competitor. Keep the conversation open and non-specific unless the prospect singles out a specific competitor.

**Explore All Options**: Keep your questions broad and neutral to learn about all the competitors they are considering:

*"I imagine there are a few options you're evaluating right now. Could you share which ones you're considering? That will help me understand how they compare with what we offer."*

**Stay Neutral**: Don't focus on any single competitor unless the prospect mentions just one. Instead, position your solution by highlighting what makes you stand out:

*"Each solution brings something to the table. Based on what you've shared, I think our offering aligns particularly well with [specific need or requirement]."*

This respectful approach keeps the tone professional and helps you gather insights without undermining the competition.

### 4. Collecting Key Information Casually

Sometimes, the most valuable information comes out in **casual conversations**. The trick is to get your prospect talking naturally and to extract details without making the prospect feel like they're being interrogated.

**Texting and Informal Communication**: Platforms like **WhatsApp** or informal emails can be gold mines for gathering details:

*"Quick check-in: Are you weighing any other options at the moment? Let me know so I can ensure our proposal hits the mark."*

When prospects feel the conversation is informal, they're more likely to **open up**.

**Offer Your Insight First**: Share something useful or insightful with them, and they'll often reciprocate with valuable details:

*"Based on projects we've worked on recently, here's what I suggest. Let me know if that aligns with your thinking so far."*

This approach keeps the conversation flowing and helps you gather details in a **natural** way.

### 5. Reading the Buying Signals

Once you've gathered key information, you need to understand whether your prospect is serious about moving forward or is still in the exploratory phase.

**Clear Buying Signals**: If they start discussing **timelines**, **stakeholders**, or **next steps**, they are likely serious about moving forward and closing the deal.

**Hesitation or Deflection**: If they keep deflecting questions about budget or competitors, they might still be in the **early stages** of decision-making. In this case, it is important to keep the conversation going and maintain the relationship without pushing too hard.

## CLOSING THOUGHT

Gathering critical information like **budget**, **competitor details**, and **timelines** requires finesse. By using smart, well-timed questions and building trust first, you can extract the information you need without making the prospect feel uncomfortable. When you approach each conversation with **empathy** and a desire to truly understand their needs, you'll find that prospects are more than willing to share the details that will help you close the deal.

Section IV

# THE EVOLVE PHASE

27

# The Power Trio: IQ, XQ, and EQ in Sales

"It's not just what you know, but how you execute and connect that makes you a top salesperson."

Sales success isn't just about knowledge or charm—it's about combining the right mix of **intelligence**, **execution**, and **emotional awareness**.

The most effective salespeople—the top 20%—stand out not only because of their ability to understand their product (IQ), but also because they know how to **execute a plan** (XQ), and most important, they know how to **connect with people** (EQ). In this chapter, we'll dive deep into the power trio of **intelligence quotient (IQ)**, **execution quotient (XQ)**, and **emotional quotient (EQ)**, with a focus on how **emotional intelligence** can make or break your sales approach.

You know your product inside out (**IQ**), you can execute your strategy flawlessly (**XQ**), and most important, you can connect with people on an emotional level to earn their trust (**EQ**). Salespeople who master all three are successful not only in closing deals but also in **building long-term relationships** with clients.

## IQ: KNOWING YOUR PRODUCT INSIDE OUT

Your **IQ** is your knowledge base—the technical understanding of your product, market trends, and the challenges your clients face. This is the **foundation** of any salesperson's skill set, and it is essential for these reasons:

- You need to **understand the client's problem** to offer a valuable solution.
- You must be able to **speak confidently** about your product's features, benefits, and limitations.

However, while **IQ** is crucial, it is not enough on its own. Many salespeople fall into the trap of thinking that knowing everything about their product is what closes deals. But the reality is that it is only the starting point.

## XQ: TURNING KNOWLEDGE INTO ACTION

Execution is what separates the **good** from the **great**. You can have all the knowledge in the world, but if you don't know how to **execute a sales strategy** effectively, it won't matter. **XQ** is about:

- **Planning**: Setting clear goals for each interaction with a prospect;

- **Persistence**: Following up strategically, without being pushy, to move the sale forward;
- **Problem-solving**: Adapting quickly and offering a solution when challenges arise during the sales process.

**XQ** is also about **consistent action**—following through with promises, sending proposals on time, and taking the right steps to turn a lead into a closed deal. However, **IQ** and **XQ** alone can feel too mechanical if you don't have the right emotional approach, and that's where **EQ** comes in.

## EQ: THE SECRET TO CLOSING DEALS

**EQ** is the real **game changer** in sales. It is the ability to **read your client's emotions**, adapt to their needs, and build a relationship based on trust. A salesperson with a strong EQ knows that people don't just buy products—they buy from **people they like and trust**.

- **Reading Emotional Cues**: Whether it is body language, tone of voice, or hesitation in a virtual call, emotional intelligence helps you **read between the lines**. If a prospect seems hesitant, it is likely they have unspoken concerns that you can address by probing gently.
- **Adapting to Different Personalities**: Every client is different. Some are more analytical and want data, whereas others are driven by emotion. **EQ allows you to adapt** your style to meet the client's emotional needs. You can't approach every client the same way, and EQ gives you the flexibility to change gears as needed.

- **Building Trust and Rapport**: People buy from those they trust. EQ enables you to build a **genuine connection** with your clients, making them feel heard and valued. This connection is often the difference between closing a deal or losing it to a competitor.

## THE THREE LEVELS OF QUESTIONING: UNCOVERING THE CLIENT'S TRUE NEEDS

A highly effective salesperson uses different **levels of questions** to engage prospects and uncover their needs. The trick is knowing when to use each level and how to guide the conversation.

- **Preliminary Questions**: These are **ice-breakers**, simple questions to gather initial information:
  *"What's the biggest challenge your team is facing right now?"*
- **Clarifying Questions**: These questions dig deeper into specific details, allowing you to understand the prospect's situation more clearly:
  *"Can you tell me more about why this challenge is a priority now?"*
- **Personal/Emotional Questions**: These questions tap into the **emotional drivers** behind the decision-making process:
  *"How would solving this problem affect your day-to-day operations?"*

By moving through these levels of questioning, you can uncover both the **logical reasons** (solving problems) and

**emotional reasons** (reducing stress, gaining control) that will motivate your prospect to make a decision.

## ADOPTING AN INCREMENTAL MINDSET

The best salespeople don't just have natural talent—they have an **incremental mindset**. They believe that intelligence, execution, and emotional intelligence can be developed over time through **effort and learning**. You don't have to be born with high EQ or XQ. Instead, you can cultivate it by:

- **Seeking Feedback**: After each sales call, ask yourself what worked, what didn't, and how you can improve. Over time, this reflection will sharpen your EQ.
- **Learning from Rejection**: Every "no" is an opportunity to learn and get better. By analyzing why a deal didn't close, you can improve your approach the next time.

## CLOSING THOUGHT

While IQ and XQ are important, it's EQ that often tips the scales in your favor. To truly excel in sales, you need to combine knowledge, execution, and emotional intelligence. **IQ** gets you in the door, **XQ** keeps the process moving, but it's **EQ** that closes the deal. By developing your emotional intelligence and combining it with the right knowledge and execution, you can elevate yourself into the top 20% of sales professionals.

# 28

# You Don't Know What You Don't Know: The Art of Educated Selling

"Great salespeople don't just pitch—they reveal what the prospect never realized they were missing."

## THE HIDDEN GAP MOST PROSPECTS MISS

One of the most powerful realizations I've had in sales is this: **"You don't know what you don't know."** And that's the silent reality for most prospects.

They may be managing their operations well on the surface—but deep down, inefficiencies, outdated systems, or legacy habits could be silently costing them time, money, and productivity. The problem is that they aren't always aware of it.

This is where a seasoned salesperson can stand out—not by pushing harder, but by **educating smarter**.

## THE POWER OF A 360-DEGREE PROSPECT STUDY

To uncover these blind spots, you must study the prospect from all angles. Understand their business model, operational gaps, internal structure, and stakeholders and personalities. You'll be surprised by how much you can uncover that even the prospect hasn't noticed.

This knowledge allows you to lead the conversation differently. Instead of "Here's what we offer," you can say, "Here's where your current system might be silently draining value." Instead of selling features, you reveal bleeding areas that need fixing.

## SELLING THE "BLEEDING VALUE" BEFORE ROI

ROI is great, but it's usually **after** implementation. How do you convince someone **before** they become a client?

You introduce the idea of **"bleeding value"** by saying something like this sentence:

*"If you continue with your current setup for another six months, here's the potential loss in man-hours, missed insights, or inefficiencies."*

That information alone can shake up a prospect more than any glowing testimonial.

## IT'S NOT ABOUT THE QUANTITY OF LEADS—IT'S ABOUT THE QUALITY OF EFFORT

People often think more leads mean more chances. But here's the truth: Even if you take **just three good leads**, study them deeply, tailor your pitch precisely, and close **just one**, you've achieved a **33% conversion rate.**

That's the kind of smart selling that scales. It's not about how many doors you knock on; it's about how well you've prepared before ringing the bell.

## DECODING THE PERSONA OF THE POINT OF CONTACT

Understanding your buyer's context is critical. Here's how different personas should shape your pitch:

- **New Joiner:** They want to prove themselves. Position your solution as a **quick win** that they can show to their management.
- **Veteran Employee:** They know the internal dynamics and politics. Respect their experience and use it to co-create a solution.
- **Mid-Level Manager:** They need backing from above. Equip them with ammunition to sell your product internally.
- **Decision-Maker:** Get straight to the point—demonstrate cost savings, efficiency, or competitive edge clearly.

**Different strokes for different folks.** That's how impactful sales works.

## EXERCISE: HOW WELL DO YOU KNOW YOUR PROSPECT?

**Goal:** To help you assess how deeply you understand your prospects before pitching

**Instructions:** Take any **three live leads** from your pipeline. For each one, answer the following questions:

### Part A: Prospect Business Understanding

- What is their core business model and revenue stream?
- What recent challenge or industry trend might be affecting them?
- Who are their direct competitors?
- What tools or processes are they currently using (that you're trying to replace or enhance)?

### Part B: Internal Persona Mapping

- Who is your point of contact, and how long have they been in the company?
- What might be their internal goal or pressure point right now?
- Are they the decision-maker or an influencer?
- What other departments or stakeholders will be involved in the decision?

### Part C: Value Positioning

- What part of their current workflow is bleeding value?
- Have you quantified the potential risk of inaction?

- Can you name at least two ways your solution can directly improve their business outcomes?
- What emotional angle (fear of missing out, ease of use, reputation gain) might resonate best?

### Scoring:

**10+ answers clear and specific:** You're ready to pitch!

**8–10 questions answered but with guesswork:** You need deeper prep.

**<10 or mostly vague responses:** Rethink your approach before contacting them.

### Reflection Prompt:

**"Did I really study my prospect, or am I just hoping they'll figure out the value on their own?"**

Remember, great sales happen when preparation meets empathy.

### CLOSING THOUGHT

A great salesperson isn't just a persuader—they're a mirror and a flashlight. They reflect what's wrong and illuminate what's possible.

So, the next time you're on a call or in a meeting, don't just pitch a product—**reveal a truth** your prospect didn't even know they needed to hear.

Once they see what they didn't know, they'll never look at their problem—or your solution—the same way again.

# 29

# The Power of Pre-indoctrination in Sales

"Set the stage before the show begins—win your prospect's mind before they even step into the buying conversation."

Pre-indoctrination in sales is about shaping your prospect's mindset **before** they engage in a serious buying conversation. It is an often-underutilized strategy that ensures your prospect is already leaning toward your solution, even before the actual sales pitch begins. Think of it as planting seeds that will sprout during the main presentation, making the final sale smoother and more predictable.

In this chapter, we'll dive deep into what pre-indoctrination is, why it is so powerful, and how you can use it to gain an edge in every sales conversation.

## WHAT IS PRE-INDOCTRINATION?

Pre-indoctrination refers to **preparing your prospect's mindset** such that they have favorable feelings toward your brand or solution by the time you're ready to formally pitch your product or service.

**Why It Works**: People are more likely to buy when they've already been primed to believe that your solution is the right one for them. When the groundwork is laid beforehand, your actual sales pitch becomes a matter of validation rather than persuasion.

**Subtle Influence**: Pre-indoctrination involves **subtly influencing** your prospect's perception before they even realize they're being sold to. By the time they enter a formal sales conversation, they are already aware of your product's value, your company's strengths, or even the pain points your product addresses.

### Why Pre-indoctrination Is a Game Changer in Sales

- **Reduced Resistance**: One of the biggest challenges in sales is overcoming resistance. Prospects often enter sales conversations with objections and doubts. Pre-indoctrination reduces resistance by addressing common objections and **positioning your product favorably** before the formal conversation begins.
- **Emotional Priming**: Sales are heavily influenced by emotion. Pre-indoctrination sets an **emotional tone** for the sales conversation, creating a feeling of trust and credibility early on.

- **Positioning as the Expert**: By the time you speak to the prospect, they should already see you as an **expert** in the field. Pre-indoctrination sets the stage for you to be seen as a trusted advisor rather than just another salesperson.

### How to Use Pre-indoctrination in Sales

There are several effective ways to use pre-indoctrination to your advantage. Let's explore the most powerful methods:

#### a. Content Marketing and Thought Leadership

**Why It Works**: By creating and sharing **valuable content**, you position yourself and your company as experts in the industry. Prospects consume this content in their own time and start building a relationship with you before any direct interaction.

**How to Use It**: Share blog posts, whitepapers, or case studies that address key challenges your prospects face. This information primes them to see you as the solution even before you reach out for a direct conversation.

**Example**: If you're selling a B2B solution, publishing an article about the "Top 5 Common Mistakes Businesses Make When Choosing a Vendor and How to Avoid Them" can indoctrinate prospects to believe that you understand the challenges they face when making important purchase decisions.

#### b. Subtle Social Proof

**Why It Works**: People trust other people's experiences. If a prospect sees testimonials, success stories, or high-profile clients who've had success with your product, they are more likely to trust you.

**How to Use It**: Present subtle but effective social proof on your website, through emails, or via marketing materials. Include client testimonials, case studies, or even a simple logo strip showing companies that trust you.

**Example**: Send an email to a prospect before your pitch that includes a case study of a similar client, explaining how your solution solved a similar problem for them.

### c. Strategic Email Sequences

**Why It Works**: Email sequences that are well crafted can influence a prospect's mindset. Through a series of nurturing emails, you can **educate**, **inform**, and **shape expectations**.

**How to Use It**: Send a sequence of three to five emails to the prospect in the days leading up to a meeting. These emails should not be about your product directly, but about the problems your product solves, industry insights, or even challenges your prospect is facing.

**Example**: Send an email sequence that starts with an industry insight, follows up with a case study, and ends with a testimonial. By the time you meet, the prospect already feels educated and primed to hear your solution.

### d. Pre-meeting Materials

**Why It Works**: Sending materials ahead of time gives the prospect something to think about before your actual meeting. It subtly frames the conversation in your favor.

**How to Use It**: A day or two before a meeting, send over a short brief that outlines the key pain points and solutions you plan to discuss. This overview primes the prospect to focus on those challenges and prepares them for your solution.

**Example**: "Ahead of our meeting, here's a brief summary of some key challenges we've identified in your industry and how we've helped other companies solve them."

## PRE-INDOCTRINATION IN ACTION: HOW IT PLAYS OUT IN THE SALES PROCESS

Let's break down how pre-indoctrination fits into the overall sales process.

**Before the First Call**: Use content marketing and subtle social proof to create awareness and credibility. By the time the prospect reaches out to you, they've already seen your content, read your blog, or watched a video about how you've helped others.

**Pre-meeting Strategy**: Send educational materials, relevant case studies, or strategic emails to start shaping the narrative before you meet. This information primes the conversation in your favor.

**During the Meeting**: The conversation becomes much smoother when you've pre-indoctrinated the prospect. They are more open to your solutions because they've already been conditioned to see the value you bring.

**Follow Up With Reinforcement**: After the meeting, send a follow-up that reinforces the positive emotions and ideas you've already seeded. This touchpoint can include additional case studies, testimonials, or a short video showcasing your product in action.

## PRE-INDOCTRINATION IS NOT MANIPULATION—IT IS EDUCATION

Pre-indoctrination is often misunderstood as a manipulative tactic. In reality, it is about **educating your prospects** so they can make informed decisions. You're not tricking anyone into buying your product—you're simply **preparing them** with the right information and perspective so they can see the full value of your solution.

- **Aligning Expectations**: Pre-indoctrination sets clear expectations and makes sure that prospects understand how your product aligns with their needs.
- **Building Trust**: By providing value up front, you build trust with the prospect before asking them to buy anything.

## PRE-INDOCTRINATION AND LONG-TERM SALES SUCCESS

Pre-indoctrination is a long-term strategy, used not just to **close a single deal**, but to **build a reputation** and a pipeline of prospects who are preconditioned to trust your company and solution.

- **Brand Consistency**: Ensure that your messaging is consistent across all platforms—your website, social media, and email communications should all reinforce the same core values and solutions. This long-term pre-indoctrination builds a strong brand identity in the minds of prospects.
- **Creating Loyal Customers**: Prospects who are pre-indoctrinated and educated are more likely to become loyal customers. They don't see you as just a vendor—they see you as a partner who genuinely understands their needs.

## CLOSING THOUGHT

Pre-indoctrination is a **powerful tool** that can transform the way you sell. By shaping the narrative and setting expectations before you even pitch your solution, you reduce objections, build trust, and increase the chances of closing the deal. Sales is no longer about convincing—it's about preparing the prospect to see the value in what you offer, long before the formal conversation begins.

If you can master the art of pre-indoctrination, you'll find that prospects aren't just willing to listen—they're ready to buy.

# 30

# *Seabiscuit*: A Movie Every Sales Professional Should Watch

"It's not the size of the horse in the race, but the size of the heart and strategy behind it."

*Seabiscuit,* directed by Gary Ross and based on the true story of a small horse that became a symbol of hope during the Great Depression, is a remarkable film that resonates deeply with sales professionals. The story of *Seabiscuit* is not just about horse racing; it is about resilience, determination, strategy, and teamwork—all vital ingredients for success in sales.

## PLOT OVERVIEW

The movie is set during the Great Depression, a time when the American spirit was low and people were looking for something to believe in. The film tells the story of three broken men—a businessman, a horse trainer, and a jockey—who come together to transform Seabiscuit, an undersized and underestimated racehorse, into a champion.

**Charles Howard** is a successful businessman who lost his son in a tragic accident. He sees potential in Seabiscuit and buys him despite the horse being written off as too small and lazy for professional racing.

**Tom Smith** is a horse trainer with unconventional methods who believes in the spirit of horses rather than their outward appearance. He sees something special in Seabiscuit that no one else does.

**Red Pollard** is a jockey with a troubled past and a body too battered for most people to bet on. But his deep connection with Seabiscuit and their shared underdog status drives him to become the horse's perfect rider.

Together, these three men defy all odds to make Seabiscuit one of the most successful racehorses in history. The journey is not without challenges—there are injuries, doubts, and losses along the way—but through perseverance, strategy, and belief in one another, they emerge victorious.

## LESSONS FOR SALES PROFESSIONALS

### Resilience in the Face of Doubt

Just as Seabiscuit was written off because of his size, many salespeople find that their ability to close deals is doubted by clients or their own teams. In sales, you will encounter rejection, tough competition, and moments where everything seems to be going against you. The key is to stay resilient, keep pushing forward, and believe in your potential—just like Seabiscuit and his team did.

**Sales Takeaway**: Never let initial setbacks or external doubts define your journey. In sales, success often comes from pushing through the hardest challenges with unwavering determination.

## THE POWER OF STRATEGY

Seabiscuit didn't win just because he was fast. He won because his trainer, Tom Smith, understood how to leverage the horse's strengths while compensating for his weaknesses. They carefully chose races where Seabiscuit's endurance and racing style would give him an edge, and the strategy paid off. Similarly, in sales, you can't rush into every deal with the same approach—you need to understand the landscape, know your competition, and apply strategies that play to your strengths.

**Sales Takeaway**: Tailor your sales strategy based on the specific deal, competition, and client. A well-thought-out approach will give you a strategic edge in even the toughest markets.

## TEAMWORK AND COLLABORATION

One of the most heartwarming aspects of *Seabiscuit* is the teamwork between Howard, Smith, and Pollard. Each brought a unique skill set to the table—Howard with his business acumen, Smith with his understanding of horses, and Pollard with his tenacity as a jockey. It is their combined effort that leads Seabiscuit to greatness. In sales too, it is critical to recognize that you can't always do it alone. You need to collaborate with your sales team, product experts, and marketing folks, for a combined effort can lead to more successful outcomes.

**Sales Takeaway**: Leverage the power of teamwork. In complex sales, collaboration with cross-functional teams can help you bring in more expertise, create stronger proposals, and close deals faster.

## BELIEVING IN THE UNDERDOG

Seabiscuit's journey is about believing in the underdog. Despite all odds, the horse goes on to beat more established and favored competitors. In sales, you might not always have the biggest product or the most well-known brand, but belief in yourself, your product, and your team can help you win deals that seem out of reach.

**Sales Takeaway**: Even if you're not selling the "market leader," you can win by positioning your offering as the best fit for your customer. Use your unique strengths to your advantage, and always believe in your ability to outperform bigger players.

## TURNING SETBACKS INTO COMEBACKS

There are multiple setbacks in Seabiscuit's journey, including a career-threatening injury to the horse. Rather than giving up, however, the team allows Seabiscuit to rest, recover, and return even stronger. This mirrors the sales process—sometimes, a deal may go cold, or a client may reject your initial pitch. Instead of walking away, it's essential to regroup, learn from the setback, and come back with an even better strategy.

**Sales Takeaway**: A rejection isn't the end. Use setbacks as learning opportunities to refine your approach and come back stronger. Persistence, combined with a renewed strategy, is the key to long-term success.

## THE UNDERDOG MENTALITY: EMBRACE CHALLENGES

Seabiscuit thrived as the underdog, overcoming more powerful horses and showing that size doesn't matter. In sales, this mentality can be incredibly powerful. You may not always have the largest market share or the most recognized brand, but you can win by being nimble, responsive, and dedicated.

**Sales Takeaway**: Sales is often about outsmarting the competition, not outspending them. When you embrace the underdog mentality, you push harder and adapt faster, which can help you secure deals that seem impossible.

## CLOSING THOUGHT

Watching *Seabiscuit* offers powerful parallels to the sales journey. Sales isn't just about closing deals; it's about overcoming obstacles, strategizing, and working as a team to achieve seemingly impossible goals. The movie's message of resilience, heart, and smart strategy is a lesson every sales professional can benefit from. When you're faced with a tough quarter, a difficult client, or fierce competition, remember the story of Seabiscuit and how perseverance and belief in your abilities can lead to victory.

*Seabiscuit* is more than a film about horse racing—it's a masterclass in how grit, strategy, and teamwork can turn an underdog into a champion. Just like in sales, it's not always about being the biggest or the best known; it's about adapting, strategizing, and connecting with your prospects to win.

31

# Success Story: Winning Five Deals Worth INR 1.10 Crore by Channelizing an SI

"Genuine communication, emotional intelligence, and strategic channeling turn SIs into long-term partners, driving success for both parties."

### THE CHALLENGE:

Working with SIs and partners often involves navigating their internal dynamics and procurement processes. They bring valuable opportunities by packaging your solution with others, but at the same time, they often drag you through cycles of discount requests and endless follow-ups.

In this case, I submitted **six to seven proposals** through an SI. While they had already won two projects, we hadn't yet received the POs. Each time we followed up, the SI's procurement team pushed back, saying, "Your pricing is too high," which I suspected was just a tactic to drive further discounts.

## THE EMOTIONAL INTELLIGENCE FACTOR:

At this point, emotional intelligence (EQ) became crucial. Rather than reacting to the constant pushback and unnecessary delays, I paused to understand the **deeper motivations** at play. Procurement wasn't just focused on pricing—they were playing a strategic game, using the client's delays as leverage. My emotional intelligence helped me **remain calm and composed**, even when frustration could have set in. I knew that losing my patience wouldn't win the deal, but strategic communication might.

This was the first key realization: **Don't let their tactics disrupt your emotional balance**. The second realization came from leveraging relationships—by establishing rapport with another project manager on the team, I uncovered the real reason for the delays: The client had yet to give the green light for the project. This insight changed the entire dynamic.

## THE APPROACH:

### Step 1: Strategic Call Setup

Rather than letting the procurement team continue to play their game, I initiated a **joint call** with the SI and their procurement team. My goal wasn't just to push for the POs, but to address the underlying issues that were causing these delays. The **emotional intelligence** here was understanding that an aggressive approach wouldn't work—I needed to manage their perceptions and guide the conversation in a way that fostered openness and honesty.

I set the agenda for the call: We would discuss the multiple projects they had won and the reasons behind the delayed POs. By positioning myself as a partner who was **genuinely trying to help** them succeed, I defused the tension.

### Step 2: Building Leverage With Emotional Intelligence

During the call, I acknowledged the long-term partnership we were building and the visibility of winning **four or five more deals** together. But I didn't shy away from addressing the real issue.

I said, "I've been genuine and responsive with your team, but I'm a bit disappointed that procurement keeps pushing back, saying our price is too high when we both know that's not the case. We have contacts with the same clients, and I've done my background work—other SIs have told us the same thing. The projects are delayed on the client's side."

This was a **strategic use of emotional intelligence**. I wasn't blaming anyone, but I made it clear that I wasn't going to let them continue their tactics. By acknowledging their position and showing empathy, I created an atmosphere where they felt safe to be honest.

### Step 3: Addressing the Procurement Team's Games With Calm Assertiveness

Now came the moment to address the procurement representative who had been pushing for discounts. With calm assertiveness,

I said, "Your target price will always be lower than our quoted price, and I understand that. But I also know the margins you've kept on top of our transfer price. Let's stop this running around and be up front with each other."

Then, I used my **XQ** by shifting to a solution-focused approach: "If your goal is to achieve more savings, just tell me. We'll figure something out. But constantly asking for discounts at every stage forces us to keep a buffer, and that's not beneficial for anyone. I'm offering you the best price, 30% less than what we typically quote to others. However, to lock in this price, I need the PO issued within two weeks."

This approach combined **EQ and XQ**—I addressed their emotional need to feel like they were achieving their KPIs while simultaneously pushing for actionable results with a deadline.

### Step 4: Building Trust and Offering Value to the SI

In the midst of these discussions, I also recommended this **particular SI to some of our clients** who needed their offerings. This was a key move because it **fostered a deeper partnership**, showing the SI that we were invested in their success as well. When procurement learned about this, they realized it was already a **win-win situation** for both sides. The **emotional intelligence** here was in demonstrating mutual benefit, which made it harder for them to continue squeezing for discounts.

Turning to the SI, I said, "I've personally handled your account, ensuring you receive fast responses and the best pricing. If you need further discounts, just say so, but we can't keep adjusting the price at every stage. It's not sustainable. Let's work together to finalize these deals."

This statement wasn't just about pricing—it was about building **trust and transparency** with the SI. By being open about how we could adjust the pricing while also highlighting the value they were receiving, I strengthened the partnership. The key was to balance **honesty with strategic flexibility**, which is a hallmark of high EQ.

## THE RESULT:

The shift in tone was palpable. The procurement representative, who had been playing games with us, **apologized** for the delays and admitted their tactics. The SI, too, began operating more transparently and professionally.

Within two weeks, we received **POs for five deals** worth **INR 1.10 crore**. The SI became a more reliable and engaged partner, and our pipeline with them grew stronger. This was a clear demonstration of how **emotional intelligence** combined with **strategic execution** can drive powerful results.

## LESSONS LEARNED:

- **Leverage Emotional Intelligence**: Understanding the emotions and motivations behind the procurement team's push for discounts allowed me to address the real issues and turn the situation in my favor. Emotional intelligence is not just about being empathetic—it's about using that understanding to create win-win scenarios.
- **Stay Calm Under Pressure**: Despite the procurement team's tactics, I stayed calm and avoided aggressive responses. Emotional control allowed me to keep the

conversation productive and steer it toward a positive outcome.

- **Combine EQ With XQ**: Execution matters just as much as emotional intelligence. Setting a firm deadline for issuing the POs while showing flexibility in pricing demonstrated both **emotional intelligence** and **executional precision**.
- **Be Transparent With Your Partners**: I built trust with the SI by being open about our pricing strategy and explaining the impact of their constant discount requests. This transparency laid the groundwork for a stronger, more professional relationship moving forward.
- **Don't Let Procurement Run the Show**: Procurement teams are skilled at squeezing margins, but by using emotional intelligence and having the right information, you can regain control of the negotiation. It's essential to build a strong rapport, not just with procurement, but also with other key players in the organization.
- **Create Mutual Benefits**: By recommending the SI to other clients, I demonstrated that we were equally invested in their success. This reciprocal approach strengthened the relationship and showed the procurement team that we were valuable partners beyond just pricing.

## CLOSING THOUGHT

This success story exemplifies the importance of **balancing emotional intelligence and execution** in sales. By understanding the motivations of the procurement team and the SI, addressing their concerns head-on, and executing with precision, I turned a challenging situation into a major win. Building long-term partnerships isn't about discounts—it's about **honesty, trust, and strategic communication**.

32

# The Power of Humor in Sales: Why Every Sales Professional Needs a Sense of Humor

"Humor is a hidden superpower in sales—it lightens the load, breaks down barriers, and builds lasting connections."

## WHY HUMOR IS ESSENTIAL FOR SALES PROFESSIONALS

Being a sales professional is inherently stressful. With targets to meet, prospects to engage, and deals to close, the pressure can be immense. This is why having a **sense of humor** is not just a bonus—it's a necessity. Here's why humor plays a pivotal role in sales:

### 1. Easing Your Own Stress

Sales comes with daily highs and lows, and how you handle the lows is crucial for long-term success. Without humor, every small setback—whether it's a missed target or a deal slipping away—can adversely affect your mental state.

Having a good sense of humor acts like a buffer, helping you **keep things in perspective**. A joke or a lighthearted comment can turn an otherwise bad day around, preventing you from carrying stress home or passing it to your team. Imagine coming home after a rough day at work, still carrying that frustration. If you don't have a sense of humor, you might unintentionally **lash out at family members**, creating unnecessary tension.

Similarly, humor helps you **navigate the work environment**. Whether you're a manager or part of the team, humor can defuse conflicts, smooth over difficult conversations, and keep the morale high even in high-pressure situations.

**Example:** After a challenging day of back-and-forth negotiations, imagine ending a meeting with a light comment like, "Well, at least we all agreed on one thing today—the coffee here is terrible!" It defuses tension and helps everyone leave with a smile.

### 2. Breaking Down Barriers With Prospects

Salespeople often face challenges in getting prospects to open up. Prospects can be guarded, especially if they've been approached by multiple vendors. Humor can be your secret weapon to **break down these walls** and establish rapport quickly.

By injecting a bit of humor into your conversations, you **humanize yourself**. You're no longer just another salesperson trying to push a product—you're someone the prospect can relate to and enjoy talking to.

**Example:** I once had a prospect who responded to my texts and emails almost instantly. So, during one of our interactions, I jokingly said, "I thought you were a bachelor because you're available 24/7!" This lighthearted comment broke the ice, made him laugh, and from that point on, our conversations became far more relaxed. He saw me as more than just a vendor—I became someone he enjoyed engaging with.

This flexibility allows prospects to open up and treat you as more than someone trying to make a sale. **Humor adds a layer of comfort** to your relationship, making future discussions flow more naturally.

When you bring humor into your interactions, prospects should start to feel like they're **missing out** if you're not around. They should think, "If he/she were here, this conversation would have been a lot more fun!" That's the kind of presence you want to build—where the prospect feels your absence. Being **serious always doesn't help**. Use humor to make yourself **memorable and relatable**.

### 3. Making Yourself Memorable

Sales is often about being different from the competition. When prospects are considering multiple vendors, humor can make you **stand out in their minds**. While other salespeople may be focused solely on closing the deal, being personable and humorous can make you the vendor they **look forward to hearing from**.

**Example:** I've had prospects recommending local restaurants when I was in their city for a meeting, all because I casually mentioned in a previous call that I was a foodie. Such little remarks make you memorable and **deepen your connection** with prospects beyond the usual sales pitch.

By being genuine and lighthearted, you make the relationship **feel more human**. When prospects think of you, it's not just about business—it's about the positive interactions they've had with you. Even in difficult or competitive situations, humor allows you to stand out as **the person they'll remember fondly**.

### 4. Connecting Through Shared Interests

Humor doesn't always have to be about jokes. You can connect with your prospects by talking about **shared interests**, such as movies, songs, or even life situations. If you can find a relatable topic, you break down the wall between "vendor" and "prospect" and transform into someone they **enjoy engaging with**.

**Example:** Imagine referencing a popular movie or a song lyric that relates to the business situation you're discussing. I've often said, "This situation reminds me of that scene in [Movie Title]," and it immediately shifts the tone of the conversation. The prospect sees me as someone who's not just focused on selling, but someone who **gets them on a personal level**.

Humor can help you **cross into the personal space** of a prospect, making the interaction more than a professional exchange. By making yourself **relatable**, you create an environment where the prospect feels more comfortable sharing, which can lead to their disclosing valuable information that helps you close the deal.

### 5. Humor Builds Long-Lasting Relationships

Clients, partners, and even prospects will **try to treat you as more than just a vendor** if they enjoy interacting with you. Humor creates a bond that makes them **want to continue working with you**, even if the price or product isn't always the deciding factor.

Think about it: When prospects or partners feel comfortable with you, they're more likely to **trust your recommendations** and **value your opinions**. If a prospect can laugh with you, they're far more likely to **share key information** and be open about their challenges, allowing you to **provide better solutions**.

**Example:** When I share stories of my love for food or a tourist spot I enjoyed, I often find prospects reciprocating with their own suggestions. This turns what could be a purely transactional relationship into a personal connection. It also opens the door for **deeper conversations**, where prospects share more about their business needs or even other personal insights that help me tailor the solution better.

### 6. Humor as a Strategic Tool

Humor isn't just about making people laugh—it's a powerful **communication tool**. It can help you **navigate difficult**

**conversations**, lighten the mood during intense negotiations, and even turn around tense situations. When used correctly, humor can put people at ease and give you the **upper hand** in negotiations.

**Example:** In a tricky negotiation, when the conversation got heated, I made a joke about how I should have brought more coffee to the meeting because of how long it was taking. That one moment of laughter turned the energy in the room, and we were able to move forward without the tension that had been building.

Humor shows that you're confident and comfortable, which can inspire the same feelings in others. It allows you to control the **emotional temperature** of the room, and that can make a big difference in **closing the deal**.

### 7. The Steering Wheel Moment: Humor and Clarity

Sometimes, humor doesn't just defuse tension—it helps to **clarify important points**. I remember one conversation where we were finalizing a set of software features for a client, including some customizations. The client asked me, "If I hadn't asked for this, would this feature have been left out?"

I responded with a smile, "Don't worry—it's like buying a car. You wouldn't be surprised if a car came with a steering wheel, right? It's a basic expectation! And if you asked me, 'Why isn't there a steering wheel?' I certainly wouldn't say, 'Oh, because you didn't ask for it!'"

The client burst out laughing, but the message was clear—there are certain expectations that come with our solutions, and we always ensure our product fits the client's needs. Humor helped me make a critical point in a way that was lighthearted yet effective.

### CLOSING THOUGHT

Humor isn't just a nice-to-have in sales—it's a **must-have tool** for reducing stress, building rapport, and creating lasting connections with prospects, clients, and partners. While sales is often about numbers, targets, and deals, humor injects an element of humanity that makes people want to do business with you. Whether it's breaking down barriers, defusing tense situations, or simply creating a memorable interaction, humor plays an indispensable role in sales success.

Remember: **A salesperson with a good sense of humor is not just selling products—they're selling trust, confidence, and a positive experience.** And that, more than anything, can close deals and build long-term relationships.

## 33

# Work Is Worship—Integrity Over Quick Gains

"In sales, your integrity is worth more than any short-term gain. Long-term success comes from discipline and honesty."

In sales, it is easy to get swayed by quick wins or tempting offers, especially when they seem like a shortcut to success. But one thing I've learned through experience is that *work is worship*, and maintaining integrity is the foundation of long-term success.

### THE TEMPTATION:

Once, I was working with a partner in the Middle East on a significant deal. We were at the final stages, and it looked like we were going to close. I had already offered the best possible discount, and the partner was satisfied. For him, this was not just a big deal but also his first successful deal with our organization.

He was excited, and I could feel the energy of a win.

One day, during a call, he made me an unexpected offer: a personal cut in the deal's margin to the tune of *USD 10,000.* He told me that he appreciated my support throughout the process and wanted to thank me personally by offering a portion of his margin. It was a sizable amount, enough to meet some of my personal commitments, and I'd be lying if I said it didn't catch my attention.

## THE DECISION:

Now, we're all human, and when someone offers you that kind of money, it's hard not to feel tempted. I started thinking, "*USD 10,000 is a big amount. It could help meet my commitments.*" But then, a thought struck me—what kind of person would I become if I said yes?

I even walked up to the mirror and asked myself, "Are you the guy who accepts such offers? If you are, then you're ugly. Nah, not happening!" It was like a reality check. It felt as if I was looking into my own soul and realizing that my integrity was worth far more than any short-term gain.

It was like being offered something that could mess up my entire professional life. In sales, we must be *givers,* not receivers. Accepting this offer would have made me lose control over my relationship with the partner. It would have turned into a situation where I'd have to worry about him using this "secret" against me later or feeling obligated in future deals.

So, I told him, "Look, I appreciate the gesture, but I already get incentives from my company for closing deals. If I take this offer from you, it would feel like I'm earning twice for the same work, and that's not ethical."

He wasn't ready to give up. "Come on, Subhash! We all have commitments. Let's work as a team. If you don't want the cash, I can get you something else—an iPhone, a MacBook, maybe even a car?"

I smiled and said, "Thanks, but no thanks. Let's just win this deal the right way."

## THE RELIEF:

Turning down USD 10,000 wasn't easy, but did I feel relieved afterward! It was like a weight off my shoulders. I wasn't tied to any secret deal, and I could look in the mirror and still feel proud of the person staring back at me. Had I accepted, I would've been stuck in a bad situation—constantly worrying about when this secret might come out and compromise my professional ethics.

## THE LESSON:

In sales, you will face temptations—money, gifts, or favors that might seem harmless at the time. But those offers can lead you down a dangerous path. Staying disciplined and sticking to your principles will always bring you peace of mind and long-term success.

It's crucial in sales to be a *giver*, not a receiver. Being a giver means offering value, helping partners, and working with integrity. But being a receiver of unethical offers only leads to compromises that weigh you down. In this instance, I chose integrity—and I'd make that choice again every time.

## THE MORAL:

In sales, you'll face moments where your ethics will be tested. It could be money, gifts, or even favors. But remember—*work is worship,* and your principles will always bring more success in the long run than any shortcut. Always ask yourself: *Am I the kind of person who accepts such offers?* If the answer is no, then you're on the right path.

# 34

# The Monk in the Market: Mastering the Dark Corners of Sales Without Losing Your Soul

"You don't have to be corrupt to survive—but you can't afford to be clueless either."

In the real world of sales, not everything is as polished and clean as brochures and demo decks promise. Behind closed doors, amidst billion-rupee deals and high-stake decisions, a seasoned salesperson often finds themselves walking a tightrope between ethics, expectations, and emotional intelligence.

And **to thrive in the long term, a salesperson must evolve into something more than just a closer.** They must become a monk in the marketplace. Not a naïve saint. Not a corrupt manipulator. They must become someone who **knows the**

**game inside out**, recognizes the gray areas, yet stays grounded in **principles** and **professional grace.**

### 1. The World Isn't Ideal—A Salesperson Must Understand It Anyway

At some point in your sales career, you will face requests for "personal benefits," hints at "under-the-table" perks, suggestions for luxury dinners, parties, or even foreign trips, situations where favors are exchanged for access or speed, and offers to fast-track deals in exchange for something "extra."

You will hear lines like:

- "This is how it works here."
- "You'll need to take care of my people."
- "Hope you'll remember me after the PO comes."

And guess what? Acting *too innocent* doesn't help. You don't have to play dirty. But you do need to play **aware.**

### 2. The Power of Accommodation Without Compromise

This is where monk-like discipline comes in. You don't need to say yes to everything. You just need to know **how to acknowledge, absorb, and redirect**.

Examples:

- If someone demands a benefit, you might say:
  *"I understand these expectations exist ... but let's close this properly and I'll figure out what we can do within policy."*
  (Often the conversation drops or becomes manageable when addressed calmly instead of denial.)

- If you don't drink or don't wish to engage in nightlife, yet the client insists on a celebration:
  *"I'll definitely join you all for the celebration, but I'll stay with a juice or mocktail—hope you'll allow me to stay sober and sane!"*
  (The prospect respects the honesty, and you stay part of the emotional circle.)

The art is in **staying in the game**—without becoming the game.

### 3. Emotion Is the Hidden Currency in Sales

Sometimes, a deal closes not because of price or features—but because the **client feels understood, seen, and valued.**

You didn't say yes to everything they hinted at. But you didn't humiliate or embarrass them either.

This emotional intelligence—this ability to stand your ground with a smile—is what builds **unshakeable relationships**.

### 4. If You're Being Pressured

Here's a seasoned way to handle it:

*"I respect your request, and I know how the world works. But I've always believed in doing things clean. That way, even if someone questions this deal tomorrow, we'll both stand tall."*

Most important, **document everything.**

If you ever feel pushed into a situation that could harm your integrity, loop in the right stakeholders, or simply step away.

### 5. The Dual Nature of Sales—Warrior and Monk

Yes, you're a warrior on the field—chasing targets and cracking deals. But within, you must be a monk—detached from short-term temptations, aware of the darkness, yet shining with clarity.

Your principles are your long-term weapon. They may slow you down temporarily, but they will protect your credibility, brand, and peace of mind.

**CLOSING THOUGHT**

"Real sales monks don't avoid the battlefield—they just fight with grace."

Walk into any boardroom. Attend any party. Handle any deal. But carry your principles like armor and your awareness like a sword.

Because in the long run, *people don't remember the discounts you gave—they remember the respect you earned.*

# 35

# Why Socializing Is Essential for Sales Professionals

"In sales, connections aren't just for business—they're for growth, insight, and staying ahead of the game."

As sales professionals, we're often told to focus on closing deals, managing client relationships, and achieving targets. But there's another aspect that's just as crucial: **socializing**. By building a strong network with fellow sales leaders, peers, and professionals from various industries, you open yourself up to learning, exchanging ideas, and discovering new strategies.

## THE VALUE OF SOCIALIZING

Socializing is more than grabbing a beer after work; it's an opportunity to gain insights into how other sales leaders and companies operate. I make it a point to meet with a few of my friends—VPs of sales, heads of sales, and sales managers from various industries—twice a month. We have a regular spot where we catch up over dinner and drinks. These casual gatherings have proven to be invaluable learning experiences, and here's why:

- **Learning Different Sales Styles and Techniques:** Sales isn't a one-size-fits-all process. I remember one of my friends, a VP of sales, saying, *"I don't do sales—I do politics."* What he meant was that through casual conversation, he gets prospects to reveal valuable information, often without their even realizing it. He doesn't pressure them directly; instead, he talks and listens. In doing so, he gains insights that help him prepare and close deals more effectively.

  The lesson? Sometimes, it's not about the direct pitch—it's about learning to read between the lines and get the client talking. This is where the real gems of information are found.
- **Gaining Perspective on Team Management:** Another friend, a sales manager, once shared how he feels that out of his team of 30, only seven or eight members regularly carry their weight. The rest seem to be "coasting." This observation sparked a conversation around how to engage all team members effectively, and I learned strategies on how to keep my team motivated, engaged, and productive.

  These aren't things you can learn in isolation—they come from honest conversations with other sales leaders who face similar challenges. Socializing gives you the opportunity to compare notes and improve how you manage your team.

- **Staying Updated With Industry Innovations:** Socializing also helps you stay informed about the latest trends and tools. For example, one of my friends told me about how his company uses an AI tool for outbound calls. The AI dials prospects, and sales executives only get involved when a stakeholder actually answers the phone. This tool cuts down on wasted time and makes the process more efficient.

  Had I not been part of these regular meet-ups, I might not have learned about this innovative solution that could transform how sales teams approach outbound calling.

## THE POLITICS OF SALES

One of the most surprising lessons I learned during these sessions was the idea of sales being akin to "politics." As sales professionals, we often focus on the tangible aspects of closing a deal—pricing, proposals, and presentations. But there's a subtler, more strategic game that comes into play: **conversation politics**. It's about using dialogue to create comfort, gain trust, and uncover key information.

One of my friends, who excels at this technique, shared how he meets with prospects and effortlessly gains insights. Through seemingly casual conversations, he learns about the client's budget, internal challenges, and even decision-making hierarchies—all without the client realizing just how much they're revealing. This is a prime example of *politics in sales*. It is not manipulation; it is about letting the client open up naturally so that you can tailor your pitch and close the deal more effectively.

## BUILDING A PROFESSIONAL CIRCLE

By engaging with other sales leaders, I've built a **professional circle** that keeps me constantly updated, motivated, and inspired. In fact, after I shared my own experience handling difficult clients and tricky partnerships, one of my friends remarked, *"Great, dude, I see you're becoming a monster!"* That kind of feedback, especially from peers who understand the challenges of the industry, is incredibly motivating.

Socializing doesn't just give you new strategies—it also builds your confidence. When you're surrounded by people who are facing the same battles, hearing that you're doing well can be the boost you need to keep going, especially when the sales grind gets tough.

## THE BOTTOM LINE

In sales, isolation is dangerous. If you stick to the same methods or rely only on your own experience, you risk becoming outdated. By **socializing** and maintaining a circle of peers who are in similar roles, you gain new perspectives, discover fresh strategies, and learn from both successes and failures. Socializing isn't just fun—it's crucial for your growth as a sales professional.

## THE LESSON

Create your own circle. Make it a point to regularly engage with other sales professionals—whether it's over drinks, dinner, or even a coffee break. Share your challenges, listen to theirs, and most important, learn from each other. This is how you stay ahead, stay sharp, and keep evolving in your sales career.

# 36

# Hunting vs. Farming in Sales: Mastering Both for Success

"The best sales professionals don't just close deals—they cultivate long-term relationships while constantly seeking new opportunities."

In the world of sales, professionals are often categorized as either *hunters* or *farmers*. While these two terms may sound like they belong in agriculture or forestry, they are crucial concepts in sales strategy. Both hunting and farming represent different approaches to sales, and mastering both can make you a well-rounded and highly successful sales professional.

## THE HUNTER: SEEKER OF NEW BUSINESS

A **hunter** is someone who goes into the market seeking new opportunities. Hunters are aggressive, proactive, and always on the lookout for the next big deal. They thrive on the chase and are often the first to bring in fresh leads. Hunters have a knack for identifying potential prospects, whether they're cold leads or hidden opportunities, and they excel at initiating contact, building interest, and setting the stage for closing deals.

### Key Traits of a Hunter:

- **Proactive:** Hunters don't wait for leads to come to them—they go out and find them. They are constantly networking, attending events, and leveraging their contacts to generate new business.
- **Persistent:** In the hunting game, persistence is key. Hunters know they will face rejection, but they don't let it slow them down. They keep pushing forward, following up, and chasing leads until they close the deal.
- **Quick Decision-Makers:** Hunters need to be decisive, able to assess opportunities quickly, and determine whether to pursue or let go. Their ability to act fast allows them to seize the moment when an opportunity arises.

### Challenges Hunters Face:

- **Burnout Risk:** The high-energy nature of hunting for new business can lead to burnout. Constantly chasing new deals without taking time to build relationships or nurture existing clients can wear a salesperson down.
- **Short-Term Focus:** Hunters often prioritize the close and move on quickly to the next deal. This approach can sometimes result in missed opportunities for deeper, longer-term relationships that could yield more value over time.

## THE FARMER: CULTIVATOR OF RELATIONSHIPS

A **farmer** takes a different approach. Instead of constantly seeking new business, farmers focus on nurturing and growing relationships with existing clients. Their goal is to deepen those relationships, increase loyalty, and expand the business within the current client base. Farmers understand the value of long-term engagement and know that great relationships can lead to repeat business, upsells, cross-sells, and referrals.

### Key Traits of a Farmer:

- **Relationship-Oriented:** Farmers excel at building trust with clients. They take time to understand their clients' needs, listen to their pain points, and provide tailored solutions that address those needs.
- **Patient:** Farming takes time. Farmers know that cultivating a relationship isn't a quick win—it requires ongoing effort, consistent communication, and delivering on promises.
- **Strategic:** Farmers are always looking for ways to add value to the relationship. Whether it is offering new services, recommending additional products, or providing proactive support, they know how to maximize the potential of an existing account.

### Challenges Farmers Face:

- **Complacency Risk:** One of the biggest risks for farmers is becoming too comfortable with their current clients and not seeking new opportunities. Over-reliance on existing accounts can leave a salesperson vulnerable if those clients decide to go elsewhere or reduce their spending.

- **Long Sales Cycles:** Farming requires patience, as the results aren't always immediate. Building long-term relationships means navigating extended sales cycles, which can be frustrating for someone looking for quick wins.

## FINDING THE BALANCE: MASTERING BOTH HUNTING AND FARMING

In an ideal world, every salesperson would have the skills of both a hunter and a farmer. Why? Because relying solely on one approach can limit your success in sales. If you're only hunting, you may be bringing in new business but failing to capitalize on existing relationships. On the flip side, if you're only farming, you may have strong relationships but lack the pipeline of new opportunities that keeps the business growing.

Here's how to strike the balance:

- **Start as a Hunter, and Evolve as a Farmer:** Begin by hunting down new prospects and leads. Initiate relationships, close deals, and win new business. But once a deal is closed, switch to a farming mindset. Start nurturing that client, offering them additional value, and building trust for the long term.
- **Set Clear Goals for Both:** Don't let your focus skew too heavily in one direction. Set weekly or monthly targets for

both hunting (new lead generation, cold outreach) and farming (client follow-ups, upsell opportunities). Having a balanced strategy ensures that you're consistently working on new business and maintaining existing relationships.

- **Leverage CRM tools:** CRM tools are a salesperson's best friend when balancing hunting and farming. Use your CRM system to track new leads while also setting reminders for follow-ups, client touchpoints, and upsell opportunities. A well-organized CRM system allows you to juggle multiple prospects and clients without dropping the ball.
- **Adapt Your Approach to Each Client:** Not every client wants to be hunted or farmed. Some clients prefer an aggressive, straightforward approach, while others need time to warm up. Adapt your approach based on the client's personality, industry, and needs. The best salespeople are flexible and know when to switch between hunting and farming tactics.

## A SUCCESS STORY OF HUNTING AND FARMING

One of my most memorable sales experiences involved mastering both hunting and farming techniques.

I had been in touch with a prospect for months, playing the role of the hunter—constantly reaching out, staying on their radar, and positioning our solution as the best fit for their needs. After several months of persistence, I closed the deal.

I didn't stop there, however. Once the deal was signed, I immediately switched to a farming approach. I checked in regularly with the client, not just to sell more but to ensure they were satisfied with our service. I proactively suggested additional features that could improve their operations. Over the next year, that client became one of my top accounts, and we expanded our partnership significantly.

This experience taught me that to be a truly effective salesperson, you can't just be a hunter or a farmer—you have to be both. You need the determination to win new business and the patience to grow and nurture it.

**CLOSING THOUGHT**

Mastering the balance between hunting and farming is the key to long-term success in sales. While the hunter brings in new business, the farmer ensures that relationships grow and evolve, leading to long-term profitability. Together, these two approaches form the foundation of a robust sales strategy.

37

# The Power of Email in Sales: A Deeper Dive Into How Email Can Save, Drive, and Close Deals

"An email can be more powerful than any call—you just need to use it right."

Emails are a strategic tool in sales. The way you craft, follow up, and respond to emails can determine whether a deal progresses or dies. Let's dive deeper into how emails can help you control the narrative, save yourself from tricky situations, and close deals that seemed out of reach.

## EMAILS: THE HIDDEN POWER IN SALES

I've always loved emails because they allow me to **think, articulate, and push professionally**. Whether it is for proposal follow-ups, summarizing meetings, or clarifying terms, email is a critical communication tool in the B2B world.

Here's why emails are invaluable:

- **Documenting discussions**: Sending minutes of meetings (MoMs) after face-to-face meetings or demos ensures that no one can deviate from the points previously agreed upon.
- **Following up professionally**: For leads, proposals, and payments, emails allow you to formalize requests and keep stakeholders accountable.
- **Providing cover**: Emails can act as evidence in case a client or partner attacks you legally. Well-written follow-ups are often **lifesavers** when people try to backtrack on what was discussed.
- **Setting tone and expectations**: Unlike casual conversations, emails help set a professional tone and keep everyone aligned.
- **Making decisions stick**: With emails, it's not just about persuading one person; the whole team is in the loop, allowing the right decision-makers to step in.

An important **pro tip**: Sometimes, it is wise to email after a call to confirm what was discussed. This written record avoids "he said, she said" scenarios, ensuring you have proof of what was agreed upon.

## EMAILS CAN SAVE YOU FROM FALSE ALARMS

In the fast-paced world of sales, a simple missed call can spiral into a big issue. Picture this: You've called your prospect multiple times, but they don't pick up. You decide to wait for a callback, but instead, an email from the prospect lands in your inbox—"I've been waiting for your call, but I didn't hear from you."

Ouch! Suddenly, the management might question if you've been diligent. Did you actually follow up? How can you prove it? Here's where **emails come to the rescue**.

If a prospect misses your call, it's always a good idea to send a **follow-up email and a text message**. You can frame it like this:

*"Hey [Prospect Name], you may have been busy and missed my call earlier. No worries, feel free to reach out at your convenience or let me know if there's a better time to connect. I'm available whenever you're ready."*

By copying in relevant stakeholders, you create a **paper trail**. This simple act keeps you covered, and if your prospect claims they never heard from you, you have the receipts. In sales, you have to stay ahead and keep your side of the street clean.

### Emails Can Make or Break Relationships: Funny Incidents

Emails require precision and caution. **A single spelling mistake** can change the dynamics of an email or even cost you a deal. Here's a humorous (yet serious) incident that happened with one of my teammates:

Instead of typing, "Hey Tim, please do the below job," it went out as "Hey Tim, please do the blow job." Yes, that missing "e" turned a simple request into an embarrassing moment!

This incident isn't just funny—it's a reminder to double-check everything before hitting "Send." Emails have the power to:

- Accidentally **copy the wrong person**, leading to unwanted information being shared;
- Mistakenly send **commercials to the end client** instead of the partner (which can cause major headaches);
- Expose **confidential information** if not handled properly.

### Mistakes and Fortunate Accidents

Of course, emails can also work in your favor. Once, a prospect **mistakenly attached the competitor's proposal** in an email to me, thinking he was forwarding it internally. That slip-up became a treasure trove of information, allowing me to craft a stronger pitch.

### Emails in Negotiations: Avoiding Missteps

Here's another **serious pitfall**: One colleague tried to complain about a team member to another colleague but mistakenly **sent the email to the person being complained about**. The damage was irreversible.

Sure, we can all rely on the Recall button, but what if the recipient reads the email before it's recalled? Worse yet, what if they take a screenshot?

Mistakes can happen, but **double-checking recipients** and contents is essential for sales professionals. One small error can derail an entire deal.

## SUCCESS STORY: CLOSING A DEAL BY NUDGING AN ENTIRE TEAM THROUGH EMAILS

Emails don't just cover your back—they can nudge an entire organization toward a decision. Here's how I closed a deal in Saudi Arabia by strategically using emails to drive urgency and action.

### THE EXHIBITION LEAD: A GOLDEN OPPORTUNITY

During an exhibition in Saudi Arabia, I met the CEO and founder of a major contracting company at our booth. He was intrigued by our product and asked all the right questions—capabilities, presence in the region, implementation timelines, and even a rough estimate of costs. After a productive conversation, we exchanged business cards, and he promised to have his team reach out immediately. I was on cloud nine.

But the true power of this lead hit me when the neighboring exhibitor overheard the conversation and commented, "Looks like you've closed the deal, huh?" I had the same feeling.

### THE FOLLOW-UP: SILENCE FROM THE TEAM

True to his word, the founder shared my details with his team, and I was soon contacted to schedule a demo. Given that I was still at the exhibition, I quickly coordinated with my team to set up the product demo and freeze the requirements. After we submitted the proposal, I expected things to move fast.

However, I noticed the responses from his team were slow and noncommittal. When I checked the email chain, I realized they had removed the founder from the loop—**a big red flag.**

## NUDGING THROUGH EMAILS

Sensing the hesitation from the team, I requested a call with all the decision-makers. On the call, it was clear that they were dragging their feet—perhaps afraid of the change that our solution represented. I highlighted the value proposition, but I could tell they weren't fully engaged.

To add to the complexity, the founder had just undergone heart surgery and was out of action for several weeks. I stayed in touch with him during his recovery via WhatsApp, showing genuine concern for his well-being. Once he returned to work, I copied him back into the email chain, and that's when things really started to heat up.

## APPLYING PRESSURE AND CREATING URGENCY

At this point, I sent a carefully crafted email that subtly pushed the team toward action. I reminded them that we had started discussions months ago, that the offer price I had given was still valid, and—most important—that we had closed multiple other large deals in their region over the last few weeks.

Then, I hit them with a critical line: *"I encourage you to consider the risks associated with delaying the implementation of a solution. Timing is everything, and other organizations in your space have already made their move."*

By sprinkling a sense of **urgency and FOMO** (fear of missing out), I made them realize they could be falling behind.

## THE FOUNDER'S FINAL PUSH

Once the founder was back in the loop, he sent an email to his team with just one line:

*"Close it immediately."*

And that was it. The urgency was there, the deal was sealed, and within days, the PO came through without any further negotiations. They had forgotten to even ask for additional discounts—**that's the power of a well-timed email.**

## EMAILS AS A STRATEGIC TOOL IN SALES

This story perfectly illustrates how emails can be used in sales for the following purposes:

- **Nudge stakeholders who are dragging their feet**: In this case, the team wasn't ready for the change, but emails helped me keep the conversation going and build momentum.
- **Create urgency**: The prospect's team was complacent, but my email introducing the risk of delaying implementation turned things around.
- **Get leadership involved**: Copying the founder at the right time pushed the entire team to act, driving the deal to closure.
- **Avoid endless negotiations**: By strategically applying pressure, I was able to close the deal without any last-minute haggling over price.

## CLOSING THOUGHT

Emails in sales are more than just a form of communication. When used correctly, they can:

- Cover your back with your supervisors.
- Nudge prospects and stakeholders toward decisions.
- Keep everyone aligned and informed.
- Drive urgency and close deals faster.

And remember, an email is more than just a message—it's a **strategic tool** that can help you win the deal, maintain accountability, and ensure a smooth sales process from start to finish.

# 38

# The Stealth Climb: Winning in Sales Without the Hype

As we near the end of this journey through the book, I want to share some personal experiences and reflections, particularly about navigating the professional world, even when surrounded by unexpected challenges. In sales—and life—it's not always a smooth ride, but how we approach each situation defines us.

## GROWING BETWEEN THE BACKSTABBERS

Sales isn't just about closing deals; it's about perseverance, attitude, and character. Imagine starting your sales career in a company, whether a startup, medium or small enterprise, or large organization. The ideal situation would be joining a company that has strong processes in place—especially for sales. The company's environment can make or break a fresher's ability to learn and grow.

I've interviewed many salespeople, and I've heard all sorts of responses that tell me why certain people struggle. Here are some examples:

- "I don't know what to do after submitting the proposal."
- "I'm good at demos but not at closing."
- "I only handle lead harvesting."
- "I rely on scripts."
- "My manager used to handle all the final stages of negotiation."

You get the point—sales is more than just one piece of the puzzle. It's a full cycle that requires mastering everything from leads to closing, and unfortunately, not every company or salesperson nurtures these skills.

In my experience, a company that allows a salesperson to learn the entire sales cycle prepares that person not just for the current role but for life. I also believe in handpicking employees who are versatile and eager to learn multiple parts of the process. When salespeople are given that freedom, their job doesn't become monotonous. They get excited about new challenges because they know they are learning the entire game.

I create that sort of environment for my team. It's also why my next book might be titled **"How to Crack Interviews."** (Yes, see you there!)

## IT'S NOT ALWAYS ABOUT FLASHY HYPE

I've seen plenty of salespeople talk big when they first join a company. They create such a high level of expectation that even if they perform well, people think, "Well, wasn't that what you promised?" The key is to maintain a low profile. Under-promise and over-deliver—that's my mantra.

There's a huge benefit in being the salesperson that others underestimate. They'll say, "Oh, that guy? He's not a big shot," only to be proven wrong when you deliver at the right moment. Keep the hype low and let your results speak for themselves.

## HANDLING TOUGH SITUATIONS

When I worked for a BPO firm, my role initially involved answering customer calls from the United States. If a customer wanted to disconnect the service, our internal rule was to transfer them to our US team. After a while, I noticed most of these transfers weren't retained. Curious, I began asking customers why they wanted to disconnect and whether they would stay if we could fix the issue. To my surprise, many said they would. Soon after, the company allowed me to handle these calls directly.

I took personal pride in every call I handled, and before long, I was promoted to floor supervisor. This rapid rise made some coworkers envious, and they began transferring the toughest calls to me—billing complaints, frustrated customers, you name it. I struggled initially, but I saw the challenge as an opportunity. I wasn't good at handling billing issues, but I learned. Slowly, the same colleagues who had doubted me began to realize I had overcome the obstacles they'd thrown my way.

## FACING ENVY IN THE WORKPLACE

Working in sales means dealing with all kinds of people—prospects, clients, and coworkers. When I was made floor supervisor, I knew some people resented my quick rise. But instead of getting discouraged, I chose to let their resistance teach me. I thanked them openly for pushing me into challenging situations, whether intentionally or not. It's those very challenges that honed my skills.

Sometimes, your journey won't be on a red carpet—it'll be full of bumps and backstabbing. But that's where real growth happens. Let those challenges mold you. Embrace the difficulties because they are often stepping stones to success.

## CLOSING THOUGHT

Sales is a world where results matter more than talk. Stay humble, keep a low profile, and let your work do the talking. A low-key, grounded approach doesn't just win deals—it wins respect. And remember, it's often those who quietly put in the work who end up climbing the highest.

39

# The Vāli Archetype: Harnessing Ancient Strength for Modern Sales Success

"Don't let your prospects become Vāli—channel their strength into your advantage before they drain yours."

In the epic The Ramayana, Vāli stood as a symbol of unrivaled strength, known for his mystical power to **absorb half the strength of his opponent** in battle. The more you fought him, the stronger he became. But here's the twist—despite his power, Vāli's downfall resulted from his inability to temper that strength with humility, strategy, and compassion.

In modern sales, the battlefield is different, but the dynamics remain the same. If you're not careful, **prospects, partners, or procurement teams can become your Vāli—draining your energy, edge, and momentum.**

The good news? You can flip the script.

You can become the *Vāli of Sales*—but with **dharma**, wisdom, and a bit of AI-powered agility.

### 1. Absorb Strength from Every Interaction

Just like Vāli grew stronger with every blow, you must grow sharper with every conversation.

Sales Application:

Turn **objections into insights**.

If a client says, "Your product feels expensive," don't get defensive—shift the lens to value and ROI.

If a competitor is mentioned, use it to **differentiate your strengths**—not to mock, but to rise.

With AI:

Use ChatGPT or other AI tools to **analyze objection patterns**, generate responses tailored to specific concerns, and sharpen your narrative with case studies and real-time data.

### 2. Don't Let the Prospect Drain You

Prospects sometimes stall, expand scope, or request round after round of negotiations to wear you down. This is when they become Vāli—slowly draining your will.

Your Defense:

Use the **SNIPER formula** to stay focused and composed.

Set **clear timelines**, limit revisions, and **anchor the conversation** on results—not just pricing.

With AI:

Automate follow-ups. Use AI to keep the tone calm and assertive while avoiding emotional burnout.

### 3. Reverse the Flow: Let Objections Power You

Vāli's power came from absorbing energy. For you, every "No" can become a refined "Yes"—if handled right.

Sales Tactic:

Dig deep into "Your software looks complex." Reframe it with demos, user stories, or "Day in the Life" explainers.

Every objection is a chance to **upgrade your approach**.

With AI:

Let AI craft **custom rebuttals** or suggest alternate narratives that align with the prospect's personality or domain.

### 4. Procurement Battles: Learn the Energy Game

Procurement teams are Vāli in disguise—they extract concessions by prolonging conversations, escalating internal approvals, and questioning value.

Sales Mindset:

Don't be reactive. Be ready with **evidence-based responses**.

Offer **time-bound discounts** or **PO-linked incentives**.

Stay firm on pricing, and back it up with market intelligence.

With AI:

Let AI scan procurement tactics across past deals. Create **preloaded responses and discount thresholds** to stay ahead of the game.

### 5. Gain Strength from Partners and Competitors

Yes, even competitors are teachers. Like Vāli absorbing all energy, **study how others pitch**, how partners position their value, and how you can use their techniques to improve yours.

Sales Strategy:

Listen to the market.

Guide your partners with **pitch kits, videos, and cheat sheets** so they push your product effectively.

With AI:

Use AI tools to compare **feature matrices**, pricing tiers, and highlight gaps where your solution wins.

### 6. Time Your Trump Card: Don't Fire Too Soon

Vāli got stronger *during* the battle. So should you.

In sales, keep one ace up your sleeve. Reveal it **not in the beginning**, but when it matters.

Example:

When the client hesitates—**unlock premium onboarding**, a limited-time service extension, or a customization freebie.

With AI:

Ask your AI tool to **predict the perfect moment** based on the email trail and buying signals.

### 7. Humility Is Your Shield

Vāli's greatest mistake was his ego.

As a salesperson, be **firm but not arrogant, strong but not overpowering.**

Sales Reminder:

- Respect competitors.
- Thank clients—even if you lose a deal.
- Let your calm confidence define your personal brand.

### 8. Use AI to Be the Modern-Day Vāli

The original Vāli didn't have AI. You do.

Use it to:

- Personalize proposals.
- Automate follow-ups.
- Humanize your emails.
- Prepare better.
- Protect your energy.

But don't be lazy.

Don't let AI drain your authenticity. **Add your touch. Add your instincts. That's your real power.**

## CLOSING THOUGHT

Be the Vāli of sales—but with dharma. Absorb everything—feedback, resistance, and market trends—and become stronger with each deal.

Control the flow of energy. Don't let prospects, procurement teams, or partners overpower you.

Use technology, especially AI, to accelerate—not replace—your human touch.

- Be powerful. But stay humble.
- Be strategic. But remain grounded.
- And most important—don't fight like Vāli. Win like Vāli.

# 40

# AI in Sales: The Present and the Future

"AI won't take your job. But a salesperson using AI might."

## BREAKING THE MYTH

There's a myth that AI is here to take away jobs. In reality, AI is here to support, empower, and amplify human potential. In sales, AI is not your replacement—it's your copilot. Those who learn to ride the wave of AI will thrive; those who resist it will get swept away.

Sales has moved beyond just giving demos or cold calling. Today, it's about timing, personalization, and execution. With AI on your side, you're not just selling—you're selling smarter.

## PRESENT-DAY USE OF AI IN SALES

### a. Communication Enhancement

Know what to say, but not *how* to say it? AI tools like ChatGPT, Gemini, and Jasper can help craft emails, proposals, and even WhatsApp follow-ups that sound polished and persuasive.

Feeling stuck in a tricky sales conversation? Prompt AI to simulate objections and help you respond gracefully.

AI can also ask **you** the right questions to help discover the best response.

**Tip:** Don't copy-paste AI responses. Humanize them. Add your tone, warmth, and context. *Let AI structure your thoughts, not speak for you.*

### b. Proposal and Collateral Generation

AI can create pitch decks, visual explainers, product overviews, and competitor comparisons in minutes.

Want to impress a CFO? Ask AI to structure an ROI-based narrative.

Want to persuade the IT head? Let AI include information security and cybersecurity angles in your pitch.

### c. Sales Automation and Engagement

AI-powered tools can automate **follow-up emails**, set reminders, and send nudges at every step in your CRM journey.

They can analyze client sentiment from their tone in email replies or WhatsApp voice notes.

You can also use AI-powered tools to automatically adapt your email style to different personas: assertive, friendly, or formal.

### d. Strategic Sales and Negotiation Support

Facing a tough procurement team? Ask AI to generate negotiation frameworks and responses.

Wondering how to present your quote tactfully? Get suggestions from AI on how to present value before price.

Upload past sales agreements or proposals and let AI compare, highlight discrepancies, and raise red flags.

### e. Lead Intelligence and Personalization

AI can help you categorize your leads better, based on the ideal customer profile (ICP).

Want to pitch to an IT manager and a facilities head? Let AI tailor your email for each persona.

For every inbound lead, use AI to build a 360-degree view instantly—encompassing company background, decision-makers, and competitor solutions.

## 2. Case Study: How AI Turned a Near Miss Into a Major Win

A mid-level sales executive from an enterprise software firm was handling a fast-moving opportunity with a leading manufacturing company. The lead came from a cold inquiry, and the client expected a quick turnaround with a customized proposal.

### SCENARIO WITHOUT AI:

The salesperson began creating the proposal manually. It took him **1.5 days** to gather feature mapping and use cases and build the price matrix. He reused a generic presentation not tailored to manufacturing. Moreover, the follow-up email had **poor grammar** and lacked personalization.

While the salesperson was busy prepping, the competitor completed their **second round of discussion**. **The result?** The deal slipped away because of delays and lack of personalization.

## SCENARIO WITH AI:

This time, the salesperson used ChatGPT and a few AI design tools from the first hour in the following ways:

- **Summarized** the client's industry challenges using AI and mapped it to their solution instantly;
- **Created** a comparison matrix with differentiators within **30 minutes;**
- **Drafted** a compelling follow-up email emphasizing urgency, clarity, and trust;
- Used AI to **generate a visual explainer one-pager** customized for manufacturing;
- Sent the **entire proposal the same day** the inquiry came in.

**The outcome?** The client replied: "Appreciate the speed, quality, and relevance. Let's move ahead." **The PO was awarded in four days.**

## KEY TAKEAWAY:

The product didn't change. The pricing didn't change. The **process** changed—with AI. That made all the difference.

## FUTURE OF AI IN SALES: ENVISIONING WHAT'S NEXT

Like the Entity in *Mission Impossible: Dead Reckoning,* AI is evolving into something omnipresent and deeply integrated—except this time, it's for good.

In the movie, the main antagonist isn't a villain in the traditional sense. It's a sentient AI called **the Entity**—a faceless, emotionless digital force that infiltrates military systems, financial markets, intelligence databases, and more. What makes the Entity terrifying is not just its reach but its **ability to calculate infinite probabilities**. It knows how any action could unfold across thousands of scenarios and can **predict human behavior, preempt responses, and outmaneuver opponents**—all before they act.

Now, imagine a *salesperson* equipped with that kind of intelligence.

In the real world, AI is already becoming a predictive force—not to threaten humanity, but to **elevate the way we sell, engage, and win**.

In the future, AI will:

- **Predict Buying Behavior:** It will tell you when a client is ready to buy, when they are likely to push back, and what message will click.
- **Analyze Micro-Signals:** AI can read pauses in emails, analyze tone in voice messages, and even detect hesitation in meetings to suggest your next move.

- **Simulate Outcomes:** It can run virtual "what-if" scenarios—for instance, "What if I offered this discount?" or "What if I delayed follow-up by two days?"—and guide you to the best possible result.
- **Run Sentiment Dashboards in Real Time:** During demos or negotiations, AI might display real-time feedback from client expressions or responses.
- **Offer AI-Based Digital Twins:** You could rehearse with an AI-powered "version" of your client to refine your pitch or objection handling.
- **Enable One-Click Closures:** Eventually, proposals might be presented through AI-powered video bots that adapt in real time and collect digital approvals instantly.

AI won't just be a tool—it'll be your **intelligent partner** that understands probabilities, context, and outcomes in ways no human ever could. The only question is: **Are you ready to harness it?**

### CLOSING THOUGHT

AI is your power suit. Wear it well. Use it wisely. Don't let AI replace you. **Let AI enhance you.**

The top 1% salespeople of the future won't just be charismatic—they'll be **AI-empowered**. And that salesperson could be **you.**

## Quick Reference: Sales Frameworks Cheat Sheet

| Framework | Purpose | When to Use | Key Focus Areas |
|---|---|---|---|
| **SEDUCE** | Collect key prospect information and build rapport | Lead qualification and early discovery | Situation, Expectations, Decision-makers, Urgency, Constraints, Emotions |
| **SNIPER** | Negotiate with clarity and confidence | Deal discussions and pricing objections | Set stage, Negotiate process, Identify pain, Present offer, Empathize, Respond |
| ***Brahmastra*** | Reveal game-changing value at the right time | Proposal or closing stage | Surprise, Differentiation, Perfect timing, Exclusivity |
| **Vāli** | Flip objections into insights and grow stronger | Tough negotiations or procurement tactics | Agility, Control, Calm assertion, Strategic reversal |

*Tip: Print this and keep it near your desk. These are your weapons to seal every deal!*

# 41

# Revisit, Rethink, and Rise

"The finish line isn't the end—it's a checkpoint for your next level."

As we come to the final chapter of this book, let's pause—not to end, but to reflect, recalibrate, and reignite.

Sales is not just about chasing targets or submitting proposals. It's about constant evolution—**rethinking your strategies, reflecting on what worked, and rising stronger** every single time. It's about learning to win smarter, not harder.

You've just been on a sales journey packed with frameworks, formulas, philosophies, and some fun. It's time to ask: **What will you do with it?**

## REVISIT THE SCENARIOS: ARE YOU READY TO BE THE X-FACTOR?

Let's go back to the thought-provoking scenarios I challenged you with earlier. Revisit them now with your newfound insights:

**Can you be the X-factor that saves your company?** When a deal becomes the make-or-break moment, can you rise like a warrior and win?

**Can you close that critical year-end deal?** The pressure's on. Everyone's watching. Can you pull off a clinical, calm closure—using SNIPER?

**Can you be the consistent closer—the sales rockstar?** It's not about one-hit wonders. Can you repeat success and build your legend?

**Can you make yourself indispensable?** When your name is mentioned, do people feel that they *need* you? That's what SEDUCE teaches.

**Can you turn the tide of underperformance?** If you've slipped or been overlooked, do you have the courage to rise again?

## THE FORMULAS YOU CAN LIVE BY

Let's recap the **tools and philosophies** that make this book unique:

- **SEDUCE**: The art of uncovering needs, understanding emotions, and building trust before the pitch begins
- **SNIPER**: Your negotiation playbook—precision, timing, and impact
- **Trump Card**: That killer move you save for just the right moment—like a magician revealing the final act

## UNIQUE PERSPECTIVES WE EXPLORED

- **Emotional Intelligence (EQ)**: Read people, sense situations, and respond—not react.
- **Execution Quotient (XQ)**: Sales isn't about what you *plan* to do. It's what you actually *do*.
- **Low-Profile Strategy**: Forget the hype. Let your work speak. Under-promise. Over-deliver.
- **The Stealth Climb**: Climb in silence. Let your victories make the noise.

## POWER OF EMAILS AND DIGITAL DILIGENCE

Emails are instruments of persuasion, professionalism, and proof. They help you follow up with precision, summarize like a pro, and protect yourself when things go wrong.

We even explored funny real-world email bloopers—and how crafting the right email at the right time can close deals, nudge decision-makers, or revive dead conversations.

## PRE-INDOCTRINATION: WIN BEFORE YOU PITCH

We discussed how to set the narrative *before* you even enter the room. Write articles. Drop relevant case studies. Post insightful content. Create the perception of value so that by the time you pitch, they're already sold on you.

## SALES IN THE AGE OF AI: WELCOME TO THE FUTURE

Sales isn't what it used to be. The smart salespeople of tomorrow are already using **AI tools** today to:

- Generate better proposals in minutes.
- Reframe complex emails.
- Prepare visual explainers, dashboards, and comparisons.
- Analyze client emotions through tone.
- Schedule follow-ups automatically.
- Tailor messaging to buyer personas.
- Practice negotiation with AI personas.
- Spot red flags in contracts using document comparison.

Remember this: **AI won't take your job. But a salesperson using AI might.**

The chapter on AI didn't just offer tech talk—it offered a blueprint for using AI **as your sales copilot**. This is your time to evolve and stay relevant.

## SALES IS A SPORT, SO TRAIN LIKE AN ATHLETE

- **Socialize**: Learn from peers, mentors, and your tribe. Ideas spark over coffee, not just in conference rooms.
- **Stay Humble**: Don't flaunt. Let your results speak.
- **Stay Curious**: Read. Test. Try new tools. Watch been on your competitors. Stay ahead.
- **Build Your Brand**: Be known for something. Let people say, "If that salesperson is in the deal, it's going to close."

## THIS IS YOUR BOOK NOW

This isn't just *my* journey—it is now *your* playbook. Mark it, scribble in it, refer back to it.

Treat this book like your **sales journal**. Keep coming back to it every quarter. Reflect on where you are, how you're doing, and where you want to go.

## ONE FINAL NUDGE

- **Don't wait for opportunities—create them.**
- **Don't fear rejection—learn from it.**
- **Don't chase success—become so good it finds you.**

## FEEDBACK IS FUEL—LET'S GROW TOGETHER

If this book has helped you even by 1%, I'd love to know.

Tag me on social media. Share your wins. Tell others about it—it might change their path too.

And if you think something could've been better—tell me that too. I'm learning, just like you.

Let's keep sealing the deals—and raising the bar.

JAICO PUBLISHING HOUSE
Elevate Your Life. Transform Your World.

ESTABLISHED IN 1946, Jaico Publishing House is home to world-transforming authors such as Robin Sharma, Sadhguru, Osho, the Dalai Lama, Deepak Chopra, Eknath Easwaran, Paramhansa Yogananda, Devdutt Pattanaik, Radhakrishnan Pillai, Morgan Housel, Napoleon Hill, John Maxwell, Brian Tracy, and Stephen Hawking.

Our late founder Mr. Jaman Shah first established Jaico as a book distribution company. Sensing that independence was around the corner, he aptly named his company Jaico ('Jai' means victory in Hindi). In order to service the significant demand for affordable books in a developing nation, Mr. Shah initiated Jaico's own publications. Jaico was India's first publisher of paperback books in the English language.

While self-help; religion and philosophy; mind, body and spirit; and business titles form the cornerstone of our non-fiction list, we publish an exciting range of current affairs, history, biography, art and architecture, travel, and popular science books as well. Our renewed focus on popular fiction is evident in our new titles by a host of fresh young talent from India and abroad.

Jaico's translations division publishes select bestselling titles in over 10 regional languages including Gujarati, Hindi, Kannada, Malayalam, Marathi, Tamil, and Telugu. These include titles from renowned national and international authors like Sudha Murthy, Gaur Gopal Das, Swami Mukundananda, Jay Shetty, Simon Sinek, Ankur Warikoo and Jeff Keller.

Visit our Website

Boasting one of India's largest book distribution networks, Jaico has its headquarters in Mumbai, with branches in Ahmedabad, Bangalore, Chennai, Delhi, Hyderabad, and Kolkata. This network ensures that our books reach all parts of the country, both urban and rural.